Gardening
F·O·R G·O·O·F·S

Donna Balzer

Publisher:

DOX 46021, INGLEWOOD P.O.
CALGARY, AB T2G 5H7

Copyright 1995 by No Sweat Gardening Inc.
All rights reserved.
Printed in Calgary, Alberta, Canada.

While every effort has been made to ensure that the information in 'Gardening for Goofs' is accurate and up-to-date, No Sweat Gardening Inc. takes no responsibility for the accuracy of the contents of this book. No endorsement is intended for products mentioned, nor is criticism meant for products not mentioned.

1st Printing May 1995
2nd Printing Oct 1995
3rd Printing May 1997

ISBN 0-9699269-0-1

Canadian Cataloguing in Publication Data

Balzer, Donna, 1956-
Gardening for goofs

Includes bibliographical references and index.

ISBN 0-9699269-0-1

1. Gardening — Canada. I. Title.
SB453.3.C2B44 1996   635'.0971   C96-910102-3

Design, illustrations and cover by
Hillary Robins-Harkness

About the artist: Hillary Robins-Harkness, a graduate of the Alberta College of Art, is a visual communications specialist. She works out of her home designing and illustrating for clients in and around Calgary.

Dedicated And In Response To:

- **M**y friends: Patty requested a book of gardening basics titled "Gardening for Goofs"; Karen insisted I get it done while she was away at Law School; Pam was a scrupulous editor; Deanna kept acting as my agent; Gail provided humour; and Pat kept me posted with questions from her new garden. The rest of the "CB's" provided moral support and encouragement.

- My family: including "the kids" (Kalen, Chelsie, and Brennan) who have tried unsuccessfully to keep me chauffeuring and away from the keyboard.

- Thanks to: My dedicated "proofers": Anne Newhouse, Patty McKenzie, Don Hickey and Anita Schill.

Planning a garden with a little knowledge helps you to avoid the common pitfalls and hassles. Failing to plant a tree correctly, or forgetting to cover your tomatoes the evening of the first big frost isn't life threatening, but it could be frustrating if you are a beginner and don't have a clue what to do. This question and answer guidebook will walk you through the common mistakes or queries made by your neighbours and friends. It should save you a lot of grief, both emotional and physical, in your own backyard. Use this guide to begin 'goofless' gardening today.

3

4

Contents:

"**B**ut our area is so special, there is no way any single book could answer everything" is a valid and just comment which could apply to almost any gardening region. In fact, some people even try to apply this logic to their **part** of town. In my experience throughout Alberta and during my cross-country television broadcasts there is a common denominator among gardeners. We are all subject to the same trendy influences; we are willing to forge ahead in explorer fashion learning new ways; and we share some of the same basic difficulties. All gardeners begin at the same place... as goofs.

Introduction: Why This Book?

I have answered gardening questions on the plane, in my neighbour's yard, in the dentist's office, and, of course, at parties. I have answered questions at lectures, on local radio, and on province-wide radio. But when I was asked to answer questions on National Television, I hesitated for the first time. I worried about unknown plants and unknown pests from unknown places. When I began a regularly televised talk-show to answer garden questions, I found out everyone who gardens has the same basic concerns and questions. In May, new gardeners want to figure out what that birch leaf thing is again, and, in July, the problem du jour is slugs. All year long home-owners are passionate about their lawns and it is not unusual to have turf questions in January or July... they just keep coming. This book was written in response to my discovery there is a core of concerns among northern gardeners. I continue to answer these questions and have decided to put them all in one place... this book.

There is new information published every week which forces me to constantly update and improve my answers. This made me wonder if there was any point ever finishing this... the updates could literally go on forever. I'll be the first to admit I may answer the question posed from one spring to the next with a new twist because new information has given me a new insight into the problem. But the common questions keep coming and I realized, if nothing else, I could present a frozen moment in time to those new gardeners needing a starting point.

This brings me to the whole world of "new" problems in the garden and "new" ideas coming forward. Insects, for instance, are mobile; the types found as pests and the types offered as cures for other pests have changed dramatically since I graduated from University in 1978.

In addition to new answers to old questions, and "new"

problems in the garden, questions arise from changing trends or styles in gardening including xeriscaping, gardening with wild-flowers, and more flexible, personal gardening styles which suit our individual lives. There may have been a clear right and wrong way to do things in the past, but today I offer alternatives and let the reader decide what is right for them at this time in their gardening career. This frustrates some people who want a step by step approach sanctioned by all. Other people like this flexible approach because it allows them to play in their garden and, using the advice in this book, avoid tragedy.

This is not an insect identification or pesticide applicator's manual. Where an insect or treatment is unique to the northern garden, I mention it and offer some alternatives. I am providing an outline for gardening more than a "trouble-shooting" manual. Do not depend on untrained seasonal staff, or over-the-fence diagnostics to plot chemical warfare against the world's critters. Take a moment to consult regional agricultural offices or the chemical company supplying the product if details are needed about insects, fungi, and bacterial diseases. Alternatively, hire help for cases of chronic infestations.

Most readers will know that proper preventative gardening and simple common sense techniques will often prevent the stresses that lead to major insect outbreaks. Other people patiently wait out the lemming-like population swings of some pests and work around these outbreaks, encouraging the beneficial insects wherever possible. Either way, the alternatives are mentioned and discussed here as they apply to the home garden.

This is a fun and casual antidote to encyclopedic volumes of in-depth study already in print on the topic. It is filled with handy hints, photos, illustrations, and tidbits of information that are fun to share at parties. I hope it is as enjoyable to read as it was to write. I also hope to hear from my readers with their comments and further questions. I've provided a response sheet which is a question sheet you may photocopy and send to me. I will include the best or most unique questions in future editions of this book.

A Message To New Homeowners

(Carry on if you've passed this "garden-initiation phase")

*T*he first thing people think of when they think "fully land-scaped" is lawn. Before almost anything else, the owner of a new home will put "order sod" on the top of their to-do list. Years later they scratch their heads and wonder, "Why did we put in such a big lawn anyway?" Then they spend a fortune removing unwanted sod as they develop their dream landscapes in the latest garden fashion.

Advice to the owner of a new home is simple... live with the dust while you plan your garden, at least in a simplistic way. Decide the main use areas of the garden first, waiting until the soil is improved and the area where the sod is to be laid has been roughly defined. Sod is equivalent to carpet. It isn't necessary everywhere, so why pay to put it everywhere? Also, why pay for wall-to-wall when area rugs will do? Laying sod vs. seeding is like buying Persian rugs if mill-produced rugs suit your budget better. And if you prefer hardwood? Avoid lawns altogether by using alternatives such as naturalized wild-flowers or mulched shrubbery.

In other words, don't buy more sod than you need, and don't buy sod if you don't want it or if you can only afford a bag of seed. Success with turf depends on the care given to primary soil preparation. If soil and soil amendments are too expensive, hold off on the lawn until you can afford them. At a cost of less than ten dollars to buy seed for an average city lawn after the soil preparation is complete, it won't be long before you can begin.

Regardless of the age of the home or status of the yard, the first real step in getting the yard you want is analysing the yard you have. Consider what is there and what is desired. Read. Start clipping photos from magazines and taking snapshots during your local horticultural society's open garden competitions. Read. Many of the solutions to a beautiful garden are right next door in an enthusiastic gardener's yard. Visit. Go to local nurseries and garden centres in the spring to see what is available. Read. Assemble your favourite ideas and don't be afraid to incorporate them later in a plan of your own.

Even with the basic premise that almost everyone wants a lawn, there is more to consider before you begin:

- What do you have?
- What do you want?
- How do you get what you want?

It is hard to tell any one person what they should have because opinions and styles vary. A good designer will help guide you through the decision making process, but you can easily do a basic inventory, complete with photos, before you go any further. Each season of the year affords some planning possibilities. Take advantage of whatever season you are in when you begin your plan. Jot down colourful plants in the current season and begin a year-long diary to make sure there is colour every time you glance out the window or stroll the estate. In the winter, a bright blue hoopsii spruce may satisfy the colour urge if your house is an estate, but if it is a townhome, try a close relative of this big spruce, the dwarf blue spruce. There really is something for every yard in every season. Still not sure? Plunge in anyway. Most gardens will be redone a few times over, so most of all, don't worry. Get started. ✎

How much soil do you need to order for a new garden? This six-foot person (right) is standing beside 10 yards of loam. A new garden might easily absorb 30 yards of soil or more.

Small plants are the best for an infill or condominium garden. This illustration of teeny plants features: (from left to right) <u>Bergenia</u>, tiny rubies dianthus, (six-foot person), poppy, gentian, sea thrift, high-graft little leaf lilac, big smile sunflower, and nest spruce.

Chapter One
J·A·N·U·A·R·Y

Thinking About Getting Started

$\mathcal{G}$iggle over the 124 pound cabbage or sigh over a new perennial as you browse through the new crop of seed and plant catalogues. Admire the new shades of your favourite flowers, or cringe at the introduction of yet another "black" blossom. What do people do with black tulips, black pansies, and black carnations anyway? Do they blend them with white blossoms to create a black and white garden?

This is the season of dreaming. From the arrival of the first catalogue to the final placing of orders or browsing in garden centres, January is a gardener's planning season. Once an order is placed, catalogues will arrive like clockwork every winter. To get yourself on the "mailing list" see the appendix of sources and start writing letters. The catalogues are a source of information and an inspiration of colour. If you are paper conscious, write for the catalogues on behalf of your local library, after first speaking with your librarian! You'll find most librarians are accommodating and helpful. They may already have a stable of catalogues on order, or they may welcome your offer to make the arrangements. These catalogues may then be used by everyone in the neighbourhood. The information will be useful regardless of where it comes from. Some foreign (read: American) companies are now making arrangements to ship to Canada without the need for each individual to get the necessary import and phytosanitary permits required by Agriculture Canada.

Does the source of flower and vegetable seed really matter? Yes and No. The genetic source matters but the production location doesn't. If a plant has been developed for straighter pods or thicker stems or sweeter roots, this will be "fixed" in their genetics. Whether the seed is reproduced in Guatemala or California or Calgary is irrelevant. The seed will be the same if the cultivar or variety of plant is the same. Where you will find differences in seed is from open pollinated stock. These seeds will reflect the differences in climate or outside factors.

Black-capped Chickadee, Parus atricapillus (left).

To Do This Month:
🌱 *Review catalogues.*

🌱 *Take a close look out your windows... do you need a new plan for the garden? Have you got enough winter colour?*

🌱 *Order seeds.*

🌱 *Start the earliest flowers, like seed geraniums, and grasses like pennisetum.*

🌱 *Build a special "growing area" for your newly started seeds.*

🌱 *Pretreat seed of perennials so they will be ready to start later this spring.*

Recently there has been a revival of "Old Fashioned" seeds. These are usually open pollinated so they may differ widely if produced in different locations or under different growing conditions. The "source" also makes a difference for seeds of wild plants and woody plants. The original source for these plants is especially important because the further north the original seeds came from, the more chance the plants will thrive in your garden in Calgary.

Some companies now offer organically grown or chemical free seed, meaning, I suppose, the mother and father plants and soil were chemical free. I only "suppose" this because the laws and definitions of "organic" are variable between provinces and between states. There are some arguments to support this use of chemical free seeds if you can actually find them. The pollen (male component of the genetics) may be affected by non-organic treatments as may the female parts. It seems far fetched until you relate it to human counterparts. Sperm may be affected and therefore affect offspring several years after the dad was exposed to chemicals. While I wouldn't get paranoid over the pros and cons of different seed sources or conditions of production, I do have a few favourite cultivars. These change as frequently as new plants come on the market and I am as likely to be influenced by the new crop of catalogues as any other single factor.

So collapse on your couch with a favourite new catalogue or two and start reading. Daydream as the redpolls or chickadees visit your spent sunflowers or bird feeder. It's a season of planning and daydreaming. 🍂

There are so many little black flies hovering around my house plants when I move them or touch them. Sometimes if the flies are seen away from the plants they look like fruit flies. What are they and what can I do about them?

You have fungus gnats. They are like small flies and are dark

Winter plants with colourful twigs/bark:

- *Coral twig dogwood - Red*
- *Golden curls willow - Yellow*
- *Golden twig dogwood - Yellow*
- *Golden willow - Yellow*
- *Mayday tree - Silver*
- *Native birch - White*
- *Native dogwood - Red*
- *Scarlet curls willow - Red*
- *Silver maple - Silver*

grey or black in colour. They seem to arrive spontaneously but usually they arrive in the peat moss as either eggs or larvae. They simply go dormant while the moss is in storage, and await the secret ingredient, water.

Fungus gnat larvae are thin and white; they eat decomposing organic matter in the soil and are especially common where the soil surface is kept wet and soggy. They definitely become more noticeable when the soil is very moist, because they reproduce very quickly under these conditions. Often in the winter, if you maintain your regular habitual pattern of watering houseplants, the soil starts to get overly wet simply because the plants don't use as much water in the relatively cooler, lower light period of December through January. Cut back on your watering right away to allow the soil to dry out more, and use a scattering of dry soap flakes on the soil surface to discourage emerging gnats. A slice of potato on the soil surface will attract fungus gnat larvae, if you want to confirm this is your problem.

Biological controls in the form of nematodes are now available for the control of gnats if the soap doesn't work. A nematode-containing product like Biovector or Biosafe (which contain the live nematodes, *Steinernema carpocapsae*) are just the trick for fungus gnats. The nematodes are almost invisible and come in a water-based solution; they go into the soil and eventually kill the gnat larvae. Nematodes work by carrying insect-lethal bacteria. The nematodes swim right into the breathing holes (spiracles) of the ground dwelling insects and, once inside, they release their bacterial mother lode. There is an obligatory relationship between the nematode and bacteria, but somehow the bacteria does not harm the nematode. It multiplies and kills whatever insect the nematode has been able to enter. Once the insect is dead, the nematode is able to feed freely. Nematodes are not very effective against ground beetles, because the hard beetle shell offers protection against nemas. Soft-bodied maggots and larvae will be nematode home and banquet all in one.

Nematodes will not kill the adult fungus gnats because only insects in the ground are exposed to the nematode and the bacteria it carries, but that's okay because the adults are short lived anyway. This great new product, available from garden centres, also works wonders on outdoor soil-borne insects such as iris borers. Water the soil well after you have added Biosafe to it. The nematodes die quickly if exposed to daylight, so it is important to use nematodes in the evening or very early in the morning.

There is also a bacterial control for gnats which is a special form of Bt (*Bacillus thuringiensis israelensis*). This is not widely available yet.

I would like to set up a greenhouse for fern production. Have you got any ideas on how to begin?

Yes, ferns may be grown in any cool, indirectly lit location. They need absolutely sterile conditions and continuous humidity. The fern spores are comparable to seeds but not exactly the same. They may be viable for a few hours or a few years, so it is suggested that you begin with as fresh a spore source as possible. If you are not able to collect the spores yourself, you may want to join a fern society (see appendix) which offers spore giveaways.

The production of ferns from spores may take a few months. First, scrub, bleach, and sterilize all containers used for growing ferns. Next, sterilize the soil mix by microwaving it for fifteen minutes. Then, fill small pots or trays with the sterile soil and pour boiling water over the filled pots. This will surface sterilize it again. Sprinkle the spore on the cooled, sterile soil surface, and cover with a piece of clean, sterile glass or rigid plastic. Alternatively, you could put the whole pot with sterile soil and fern spore into a sterile ziplock bag.

Within two to three months, the spores will germinate and grow into tiny male and female plants. Keeping these mini-plants moist and misted will allow production of seed, and later small ferns will grow. The small ferns are very tiny therefore they are more easily transplanted into small pots as a clump rather than as individuals. Let the ferns grow on for a year or two before planting them outside even if they are a winter hardy native. All ferns will appreciate a cool, shady spot in your home or garden.

My amaryllis plant has just finished blooming. What do I do with it now?

Amaryllis is an interesting tropical bulb which is usually sold in bloom or as bulbs near Christmas. One year I let mine gradually dry and die after it bloomed at Christmas and then tossed it in the compost pile in the spring. By late summer it had not started to compost and instead had started to sprout again. The long dry period followed by the hot moist compost had stimulated regrowth. After dealing with that "don't say die" plant, I investigated methods of prolonging and extending the beauty of this flowering plant. Amaryllis need the following care:

- Remove the flower stalk as soon as the flower fades.

- Continue to water the plant and fertilize it lightly for a few months after it has finished blooming.

- Place the plant outside in the summer by sinking the pot into the garden in a shady spot.

- Allow the leaves to die back before placing outside if they are starting to yellow. It isn't essential for the leaves to die back though, so reducing the water only slightly may leave you with a healthy looking plant coming into the fall. If the leaves have dried back, and the pot has been left to dry out completely, make sure to bring it indoors in the early fall and begin rewatering the pot to encourage resprouting. Amaryllis are only left to dry if you are trying to time the bloom period. The Avant Gardener describes the effect of allowing the pots to dry out: When water was withheld for eight weeks, the plants bloomed 60 days after watering was resumed; when water was withheld

Amaryllis have beautiful blooms but do require some special care to bring them into bloom again.

for four weeks, it took up to 140 days to flower; when watering was withheld for two weeks or less it took 160 days to bloom. There was no reduction in number of flowering stalks or blooms with the withholding of water.[1]

• Leave the bulb in the same pot for several years to encourage heavier blooming and a leafier plant.

• Amaryllis do not need a cold spell and do not require a dry spell for floral development either; they will bloom two or three times a year if kept growing rather than being allowed to die back.

I received a bonsai for Christmas and now I need to know how to care for it. It is an evergreen.

Join the local Bonsai Society if there is one in your community. Alternatively, take a course through continuing education or read a book on the topic. This is a huge subject, and many books and videos have been offered. Basically, you are trying to maintain a plant in a healthy condition without letting it grow. This goes against most gardening wisdom and demands a completely different approach. Plants are watered minimally, and the top and the root are pruned regularly. They are shaped to fit one of many styles which simulate the natural twisted growth of a tree in an extreme condition in nature. Think of a spruce hanging onto the edge of a cliff, or an alpine fir dwarfed and twisted by constant wind, snow, and ice. Basically, bonsai care requires great attention to detail and it wouldn't be extreme to consider reading more about their care. They are usually treated as house plants except they often benefit from a cool spell in the fall or winter.

Bonsai evergreens which are given a short dormant period in the winter with cool air and bright light will thrive. A partially heated sunroom or a small greenhouse which has temperatures

Winter plants with colourful leaves:
• *Blue chip juniper - Purple*
• *Blue heaven juniper - Blue*
• *Blue star juniper - Blue*
• *Dwarf globe blue spruce - Blue*
• *Golden pfitzer juniper - Yellow/Green*
• *Hoopsi blue spruce - Blue*
• *Hughes juniper - Blue*
• *Paul's gold juniper - Yellow/Green*
• *Tam juniper - Blue*
• *Winterblue juniper - Blue*
• *Yukon belle juniper - Purple*

---

1. <u>Timing Bloom With Water</u>, The Avant Gardener, Page 50, Vol 23, No 7. May 1991.

ranging from zero to five degrees Celsius for at least 60 days will be perfect. Mist the leaves of the small tree regularly year round to discourage spider mites and encourage the tree to hold on to its leaves.

We want to try a ponderosa pine in our prairie garden. Will it survive?

Ponderosa pine (*Pinus ponderosa*) is a bushy, long-needled pine normally found in the dry hills of central British Columbia. There is a good chance it will grow if it is purchased when it is small, mulched immediately, and protected from the wind over the first winter. I have seen healthy, large specimens in Edmonton, Calgary, and Grande Prairie which are typical northern gardening sites. This pine is available from several nurseries. If you decide to purchase one, remember they need a lot of dedicated space because they grow very wide (at least three metres across) and do not like to be underplanted at all.

A coffee tree I started from a coffee bean six or seven years ago is getting brown leaf tips and is mainly leafy at the top. I would like it to be bushier and I am wondering why the leaves fall off on the lower branches only.

It sounds like you have a couple of problems: the lower leaves are falling off and the leaf tips are browning.

Leaf tips often turn brown due to fluorine and chlorine gases in the water. Try leaving the water sitting overnight before using it or try using rain water. As well, other factors affect leaf tips: low humidity, overfertilizing, dry soil or overly wet soil. Coffee is native to the rain forests of Africa so high humidity combined with partial shade is ideal. Try misting the air around the plant to keep the humidity high.

Young plants of the rainforest have a tendency to grow straight up. A hormone is produced in the growing tips which suppresses all side shoots. By pinching out the newest tips, side branches will form.

Winter plants with colourful leaves:

- *Brandon cedar - Green*
- *Calgary carpet juniper - Green*
- *Little giant cedar - Green*
- *Lodgepole pine - Green*
- *Mugo pine - Green*
- *Nest spruce - Green*
- *Ponderosa pine - Green*
- *Savin juniper- Green*
- *Techny cedar - Green*
- *Variegated savin juniper - Yellow/Green*

Lower leaves fall off due to improper water, light, or fertility. If you are overwatering, the little feeder roots will not be getting enough oxygen. Underwatering will cause the little roots to dry out. Either way, you will be able to see if watering is the problem by turning the pot upside down and pulling the plant gently out of the pot. The roots of a healthy plant will be bright white. If they are brown, change your watering practises. If the roots are white, you may be watering correctly, but underfertilizing. Lower leaves which gradually yellow and hang on are trying to move the available nutrients up to the new leaves. They do this when they need nitrogen fertilizer. Regular fertilizing from March until October with 20-20-20, a water-soluble fertilizer, will ensure the fertility rates are good. Use half the recommended amount, but fertilize more often if the symptoms continue. Once or twice a year, water the pot heavily to leach the soil salts out the bottom. This is a good summer project.

Is there any secret to keeping *Bougainvillea* blooming throughout the winter?

In nature, *Bougainvillea* is a woody vine which begins blooming once it reaches the high light levels of the top of the forest. It needs continued bright light to bloom, so it is difficult to keep in bloom all winter long. A dry period sometimes stimulates a new flush of growth and blossom. While it is hard to keep light levels bright throughout the winter in the house, it is easy to simulate drought. Just cut back the moisture slightly during winter and prune heavily in late January or early February. This will also cause a flush of new growth, keep the plant size in check, and stimulate blossoms by the time high natural light levels resume in spring.

I received a couple of small, living trees in small pots this Christmas with the names *Pinus pinea* and *Chamaecyparis* on the tags. Can they be put outdoors in the spring? Will they survive next winter outdoors?

The pine (*Pinus pinea*) will reach an ultimate size of 25 metres in its natural habitat and the Chamaecyparis (*Chamaecyparis*) will grow to a height of 30 metres unless you have been given a dwarf variety. These plants are just not hardy in northern gardens and it is unfortunate they have been offered as living trees by major supermarket chains.

Both trees will definitely survive outside in the summer, but will not survive if left out too late in the fall. I would repot them into a decorative but well drained pot and keep them on the deck or step in partial shade during the growing season. Plan to bring them in when fall temperatures drop to minus five to ten degrees Celsius. This could be sometime in late October or well into November depending on the season. These trees will tolerate frost but will not tolerate the root balls freezing solid; the cool temperatures will trigger a flush of new growth again next spring. Each year bring your trees indoors as the temperatures drop, and use them as Christmas trees until they outgrow your ability to move them.

Remember, once these trees are brought indoors and used as Christmas trees in your warm home, they should be left in a cool room or semi-heated greenhouse where temperatures will stay between zero to five degrees Celsius for the remainder of the winter. They won't tolerate the frigid outdoor climate once brought indoors, and will also quickly go downhill if kept too warm.

Chapter Two
F·E·B·R·U·A·R·Y
Getting Started

By now the seeds are arriving, soil is being mixed and the lengthening days and sunny spells are bringing glimpses of spring. It is time to push those geranium cuttings, start pansies, prune a few shrubs or trees, and put the finishing touches on the garden plan. If bulbs have been forced they are in full bloom now. If you haven't forced any, it may be fun to go to the greenhouse and buy a few to bring home for the windowsill. It may not officially be spring yet, but we can sure start thinking about it.

Birds will come to your feeder during the coldest spells when they need extra energy. Hang suet and black oil seeds from windowsills, and enjoy this marvel of nature.

Pruning practises have changed so much in the last decade, I really encourage everyone to take another look at what they are doing and how they are approaching this once-simple garden practise. I remember when we used to say prune so you can't hang a hat on a stub. We now encourage you to actually look at individual differences in trees and to prune accordingly. By studying trees carefully, you will see where the branch collars are, and you will be able to make sure your pruning protects rather than destroys this tree protection zone. In some cases, you might still be able to hang a hat on the final cut. Drawings in this chapter feature tree branch collars. By getting to know where they are and what they look like, you will be able to visualize pruning cuts before you make them. This will result in healthier, stress-free trees, and healthier, stress-free gardeners.

If there is anyone still using pruning paint or tar or paint, I suggest they do the same to their own wounds. Ouch! What a gunky mess that would leave. These products trap decay microorganisms beneath them and simply hide, rather than prevent, accelerated decay.

Prune **only** to lightly shape older trees or to train young trees and **not** to satisfy some urge to purge. Most pruning is best left to summer, in the four to six week period just after the trees

Limber pine, <u>Pinus flexilis</u> (left).

To Do This Month:
Revive your geraniums or toss the old and start anew.

Winter prune if it is necessary.

Start early annuals like pansies, petunias, and lobelia.

Get out the sketch pad or graph paper and start putting landscape thoughts to paper.

Plan, plan, plan.

have fully leafed out and before they start preparing for fall. This will preserve the blooms on all those early spring blooming shrubs and will prevent suckering (thin, weak sprouts from the base of the tree) in the susceptible apples, cherries, Shuberts and Maydays. See also the Pruning Wheel in June which offers a seasonal overview of pruning.

How do you grow primroses from seed?

There are so many kinds of primroses; entire books have been written on this single genus. You are likely trying to grow the common garden variety perennials, *Primula vulgaris* or *Primula auricula*. *P. vulgaris* is a semi-hardy primula with tremendously fragrant blooms in the spring and again in the fall if there has been a late summer cool spell. It comes in shades of white to yellow, blue, purple, pink, and red. It tolerates a shady location in the summer garden with brighter, but still dappled, shade in the spring. It attracts butterflies because of its early spring blossoms. It will often thrive and rebloom in the outdoor garden after being purchased as a forced plant in January.

The seed of primula is light sensitive. It germinates best on the soil surface. To keep the seed moist in this exposed condition, cover the pot or flat with a piece of glass, or put the whole flat in a plastic bag until most of the seed germinates. Small seedlings may be moved to individual pots as soon as they have three to four leaves. They will bloom by the end of their first year or early in their second spring. The common auricula primulas are so easily divided they are more commonly started as divisions than seed, but the above seeding instructions will work for these and all other primulas.

Could you name some varieties of primula which are well suited to our cold climate and tell me where to buy them?

The hardiest of all primroses has got to be *Primula auricula*. It is easily grown from seed or division and has waxy green leaves which are among the earliest to show colour in the garden each spring. The best and most vigorous colour in this primula is a soft butter yellow. They are so hardy, if you start with a few this year, within a few years you will have a large clump easily divided in the spring after they finish blooming. They are now widely available through garden centres and mail order catalogues. Some equally lovely types include: *P. cortusoides, P. denticulata, P. elatior, P. juliae, P. marginata, P. sikkimensis, P. veris, and P. vialii.*

Primula denticulata is noted for its globe-shaped flower clusters in the very early spring. It is available in purple, ruby, and white. The purple is most attractive to the earliest butterflies like red admirals and mourning cloaks which may appear on a warm April day seeking nectar. Purchase these as plants because the seed is very difficult to collect and is not usually sold as a separate colour. *Primula capitata* has ball-like flower clusters similar to *P. denticulata* except it blooms for many months instead of weeks. Many primroses are offered via seed exchanges through alpine groups and horticultural societies. Over 400 species exist plus various cultivars which provide a wide range of choices.

How do you get a *Hoya* to bloom? There are two in my home. One blooms constantly and has strong, thick stems while the other has thin stems and has not bloomed in eight to ten years.

Hoya is an extremely strong-scented, flowering, woody vine of the tropics. When in bloom, you can smell it throughout the house which makes it worth the effort to bring it into bloom.

Hoyas bloom on flowering spurs, the same way as apples. Once in bloom the first time, they will continue to bloom on spurs so be careful not to damage or remove these spurs. It does sound like you have two different types of *Hoya*. It could also be that one is in a better light situation than the other. Make

Primula denticulata attracts early butterflies like the mourning cloak.

25

sure they have very bright light throughout the year with limey, well drained soil; water them only when dry in the summer and even less in the winter when the soil should be allowed to dry out even more. When keeping the plant dry, give it just enough water to ensure the leaves don't shrivel. Following the dry spell, which may extend from November to February, spring watering may stimulate a flush of flowers if accompanied by a dilute fertilizer solution. Use a balanced fertilizer which means the three numbers on the box are in proportion such as 20-20-20.

I would like to know under what conditions *Stephanotis* will bloom. We have a three year old plant grown from seed.

Stephanotis is a woody vine, native to the tropical jungles of Madagascar. It needs very high humidity, plenty of water, and bright light to bloom. Try using a dilute fertilizer in the growing season, and reduce water in the winter when light levels are low.

What can you tell me about the corn plant which I've also heard called *Dracaena* ?

First, this woody African plant looks nothing like real corn (the *Zea mays* we grow outside and eat as corn). They are not even related. The plant you are interested in produces woody stalks with four centimetre wide broad, undivided leaves. Some types have white-edged or yellow-edged leaves. They are very popular house and office plants because they can tolerate a wide range of light and watering conditions. In other words, they can be abused and still manage to thrive. If they have a drawback, it is their sensitivity to salt and dissolved gases in the water and soil. The leaf edges will turn brown as a response to chlorine and fluorine in the water or as a result of excess fertilizer in the soil. If the soil or water pH is low, there will also be brown marks on

2. "Folk Recipes to Extend the Vase Life of Cut Roses", Lane Greer and A.E. Einert, Page 86, Hortideas, August 1994, 11(8).

the leaves. Trim off any brown leaf edges with scissors and allow water to sit for 24 hours before using to let the gases escape.

When the plant gets leggy (which means the lower leaves dry and drop off), cut the stems off at various heights and new stems will sprout. This will result in a lower, bushier plant. Be patient. It may take two to three months to regrow once chopped back. Take a close look at the corn plants for sale in stores. They have likely already been cut back once.

When the soil is dry and there isn't any snow cover in January and early February, should we be watering our evergreens and emerging tulips?

Yes and No. It is still much debated whether or not evergreens benefit from watering while they are dormant. Giving lots of water in the fall is a good start. Mulching all evergreen beds in areas that dry quickly (i.e., near the south side of a home) will prevent the soil from drying out too quickly. If it does dry, the shallow roots may suffer, so go ahead and give it some water. Tulips shouldn't be watered in the winter, though, because they have a telescoping growth habit and will retreat into the ground if the temperature is cool and they haven't been watered. If they have been watered, they may grow too tall and lush, and won't be able to retract.

What is the name of the pruning book by Dr. Shigo and how do I go about getting a copy?

I am glad you asked about Dr. Shigo. He is definitely an expert on pruning and tree care, and is at the leading edge all the way. I strongly suggest his books to anyone thinking of hiring a land-scaper to do pruning, or to anyone wishing to learn how to prune. He has revolutionized the way we look at trees. Dr. Shigo encourages training very young trees so they require minimal shaping when older. Choosing the right tree for the right spot is part of the equation for success. Contact your local library, or a reputable bookstore if you want to order any of

Dr. Shigo's books or order them directly from the author. His pruning book is simply called "Tree Pruning - A Worldwide Photo Guide" and is published by Shigo and Trees Associates, P.O. Box 769, Durham, NH, 03824, USA.

Another tree expert, Richard Harris, has written an equally excellent book which is especially useful to commercial tree people.

How do you prune a Mayday to prevent suckers?

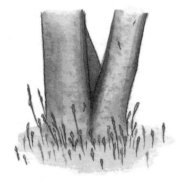

Suckers on a Mayday tree should be removed in the summer.

By not pruning in the winter! These plants (*Prunus padus commutata*) are very susceptible to suckering, especially when the top growth has been thinned in the fall or winter which leaves the over-stocked roots with energy galore. They literally push dormant buds into producing suckers in the spring. The suckers are very weak sprouts which appear at the base of a tree and attract insects such as aphids, while taking away from the nice single-trunk look of a tree. A good idea is to keep the pruning of all *Prunus* (Mayday, Schubert cherry, Amur cherry) as well as hawthorns, apples, and mountain ash to a minimum. If pruning is absolutely necessary on these trees, do it after the tree is in full leaf, starting mid-June to late-June.

If you already have suckers, wait until later in the summer to remove them. The tree will have had a chance to benefit from the energy the sucker can accumulate from the sun this summer.

Have another look at any tree in your yard that is suckering. Any tree planted too deep will sucker as a response.

How can a homeowner judge a landscaper's pruning? I am not capable of doing the pruning myself but would like to make sure I get the best possible job done.

You can start by checking to make sure you are hiring a certified arborist to do the job. Most importantly, ask for references and drive by some samples of pruning work the landscaper has completed. If you see any unnaturally shaped trees, water sprouts, suckers, or large stumps, be wary. The places where cuts have been made in past years should look like donuts, not horseshoes or almonds. Checking references and education carefully will save plenty of grief later.

Also, don't be too adamant in telling the landscaper/arborist how to do his job. Many arborists will do what you ask even if they know it is wrong just because they want to please the customer. While most reputable landscapers will refuse to top trees under any circumstances, I have heard many tales of trees being topped because that's what the client wanted. Pruning should always leave the branch collars intact. Each species has a slightly different look. Within some trees, the branch collars may even vary greatly in distance from the trunk. Once you recognize where a collar is, you will know where the cuts should be made.

Incorrect tree pruning (left) can be avoided by educating yourself or checking the education of any landscaper/arborist.

Correct pruning (right) should leave donuts.

How can you tell if a tree is hazardous?

Look for signs of decay. Does the tree have a serious lean?

29

Keep a close eye on older branches that start to turn down on mature trees. This is a sign of aging and decline. In a heavy wind, any branches that grew after a tree was topped, or any branches that are turning down instead of up, will be suspect. Check also for cracks along the main trunk, or cracks where heavy branches connect to the main trunk, and finally, look for fungus on the trunk which is a sign of internal decay. These could all be signs of weakness in the tree which will force you to do the pruning or removal sooner rather than later.

Remember, a tree is only hazardous if there is a target nearby. A tree in a forest may have all the symptoms of decay and aging mentioned above but might not be removed because it wouldn't cause any real damage if it did fall. It also provides housing for birds such as woodpeckers, or, if it falls, may provide a drumming log for ruffed grouse. If the tree with symptoms of decay is right beside a house, it poses a greater threat and definitely has a more obvious target. If the target is movable (i.e., a picnic table or bench), move the target and save the tree.

How and when do you prune evergreens to get a more compact shape?

It is possible to prune evergreens whenever the wood is not frozen. While evergreens benefit from a little trimming occasionally, it is going to be tough to shape low junipers when there is snow on the ground. If snow isn't a problem, and the branches are not frozen, trim junipers now. Repeat, if necessary, in June.

Pinch off 1/3 of the new (candle) growth on pine trees in May.

The shaping of pine, fir, and spruce is usually left until spring. These trees have a single growth spurt per year. Catching them at the right time will reduce the effort needed and guarantee the best results. Pine leaves emerge in a "candle" of new growth. The candles extend first and then the leaves appear. When the candles are almost fully extended, use your fingers to bend over the new growth and some of it will snap off. Remove about a third of each candle each year to get stocky mugo pines and compact upright pines.

New spruce and fir growth may also be snapped and shortened while it is extending. This will be in late May or early June. Don't use pruning shears to do the task because they will cut the needles, and the result will be brown, severed needles instead of more compact growth. Use your fingers to "pinch" off the extra growth in the same way the mugo pines are pinched. Spruce trees which are regularly pinched when the new growth flushes will be much more compact in the future. There will be less incremental growth allowed in a single season, so the tree will become more dense and robust.

Fig trees and many other plants can be made bushier by pinching off the growing tips.

How do you make a weeping fig tree "bush" out so it is fatter and thicker?

You pinch off some of the outer growing tips. Usually I say "pinch" because you use your fingers and thumb to literally pinch the fresh young growing tips off. These tips have a chemical in them which prevents the buds on the branch below from sprouting. Once the ends are removed, the lower buds sprout new leaves, and the end result is a fatter, thicker looking plant.

I keep seeing woodpeckers on my trees drilling holes. Are they harming the trees with their drilling?

No, the woodpeckers are not harming the tree. By the time there are enough insects inside a tree to attract a woodpecker, the tree is already on the downhill cycle. It is probably rotten at the core due to some earlier damage, and the insects are moving in to begin the decomposition process.

Woodpeckers, as well as sapsuckers, will peck at anything (even a chimney) but are likely to keep after a tree that has a food source or weak, easily drilled wood. If the tree is infested with insects, it is dying and the bird damage won't be what kills the tree, you probably will. Have a look at the tree in question for other signs of decline and decay before you make your final

Sapsuckers at a tree often indicate the tree has deeper problems.

decision. (See previous question on hazardous trees.) If you decide you have a mostly healthy rather than hazardous tree, you can sometimes slow down the sapsucker damage by hanging tinfoil pie plates from tree branches where they will clang against the trunk and reflect light to defray the birds.

A geranium has been in my basement since last fall when I brought it in from the garden. I am not even sure if it is alive, but if it is, how do I revive it?

I understand from your question you have not been "caring" for your geranium over the winter. It has been left in the basement in soil that has dried, and the plant has probably withered and dried out. In this case, you will want to cut it well back if this has not been done already. You will increase the amount of water and then gradually move it out into the sun. It will probably send out buds from where the old leaf bases were if it is not too dried out.

If you have been watering it sparingly all winter, it is probably leggy and leafless on the bottom half, but still green and growing. In this case, I would also cut it well back to a few main stems and allow it to sprout. Once it starts to grow, start fertilizing with a dilute solution of 20-20-20. This will encourage lots of green shoots. In a month, move it to the brightest light you have, preferably within 15 centimetres of a full-spectrum fluorescent light. This bright light, combined with the extra fertilizer, will bring it back into bloom by planting out time. Once it is regrowing, do not allow it to dry out completely.

My African violet is four years old and it is just too big now. Is there any way of reducing its size?

How big is too big? Many people do like to grow their African violets as a single crown plant, but it's not a rule. If you are concerned about the size though, take a leaf cutting at this point and regrow a whole new plant.

When taking a leaf cutting, the individual leaves are cut from the middle of the plant so they are neither too young or too old. They are preferably cut with a razor or sharp knife at an angle. Sink more than half the leaf's stem into moist vermiculite, and then place the pot with leaf in a plastic bag. The bag is closed for a week or so to keep the humidity up around the leaf and then gradually opened, and finally removed.

Bagging a new leaf cutting will increase the humidity.

Within four to six weeks, a small plant will form at the base of the mother leaf. At this time, the leaf will still be in the original pot, but the bag will be long gone. The starter leaf may be safely cut away and the young plant transferred to African violet soil mix which is a very light soil offered in greenhouses and specialty stores. Within a year, it should be in bloom. African violets thrive under artificial lights, so may be kept on a growing tray about 15 centimetres away from a light to get the perfectly symmetrical form so desired. Window grown plants need to be rotated regularly to prevent a lopsided appearance. Many growers continuously start new violets this way to always ensure a fresh plant for display.

My house plants are growing mushrooms in the soil. Why?

There are many mushroom fungi in the air during the summer, laying in wait for just the right evenly moist, or even constantly wet, soil conditions. Either way, you may want to water your plants less, because constantly wet soil is not good for too many house plants. Also, remove the mushrooms as soon as you spot them to prevent spores from forming and spreading. If there is a brown or white crusting on the soil surface, don't confuse that with mushrooms. It is a hard water or salt buildup on the soil and may be removed just by scraping off the top layer of soil and then watering the plant well to flush out any excess salts.

I am living on an acreage and have no trees but plenty of wind. I have built a wind fence to create some shelter and now would like to grow a few wildflowers. What would be easy to start?

33

If you have any wild areas on your property or on nearby acreages, try collecting and immediately sowing seed from plants in your area this summer. Our familiar prairie crocus, for instance, produces seed from mid-May to early June and the seed must be sown immediately for best results. Seed will grow best in an open soil that is not heavily overgrown with grass. Try burning the site this spring if there is a lot of grass and heavy thatch (contacting the municipality first for information about burning permits). Follow the burning with rototilling, or at least raking, to prepare the site for flowers. As well as native seed sources, there are a few native plant nurseries now offering the plants you want.

Wildflowers which are easy to grow from seed include native asters, columbines, *Gaillardia*, prairie coneflower, bluebells, and *Monarda*. If the wind is a problem and you want to try trees before you plant wildflowers, start with the extremely hardy shrub caraganas and lilacs which form a windbreak and make the growing of other trees more possible. A shelterbelt will do weird things with blowing snow, so make sure a newly established row of shrubs or trees is not too close to a house or road where the snow will dump.

I have a laurel leaf willow (*Salix pentandra*) approximately three years old that does not appear to have rooted well. Consequently, it is leaning at about a 45 degree angle. It requires some major pruning and we're not sure how best to tackle this problem. It is approximately six to eight metres high. Any help would be appreciated.

You don't mention if you are in town or in the country. This could make a major difference. A tree at such an extreme angle that has grown so quickly will surely be weak and pose a danger to any nearby building. If it is far away in a shelterbelt somewhere, it is not posing much of a risk and may benefit from being cut back drastically. Using your own common sense, you will have to decide if it is worth saving.

I suspect it was fertilized and watered heavily to produce such dramatic growth. While a metre or two is normal in the first year, young suckers are usually cut back somewhat after the first year to encourage side branches and strengthening of the main trunk. They may also be staked at this point to encourage upright growth. If in doubt about the danger this tree poses, cut it back and start again. Winter is a good time to take cuttings. They can then be stuck in the ground in the spring after being stored as 30 centimetre long whips wrapped in plastic and left in the crisper of the fridge. Make sure to limit fertilizer in the future to prevent excessive, weak growth.

Please recommend a plant I can use as a hedge that meets the following criteria:

- **dense enough to use as a privacy barrier;**

- **grows one-and-a-half to two metres tall;**

- **will do well in an eastern exposure;**

- **won't take more than five years to mature.**

Try one of the excellent edible cherries such as Nanking cherry (*Prunus tomentosa*) or Mongolian cherry (*Prunus fruticosa*). Alternately, gooseberry (*Ribes* species) or currant (*Ribes* species) would work. I also like coral twig dogwood (*Cornus alba sibirica*) or Saskatoon (*Amelanchier alnifolia*) where the hedge can be left in a "natural" form.

You didn't say how much width you have, or whether you are interested in letting your hedge go natural but if a two metre wide hedge is okay, dogwood will reward you with excellent winter colour and lush green colour all summer. It is essential to start with small dogwood liners or seedlings rather than large potted shrubs when attempting this hedge style.

If you would like blossoms, try shrubby potentilla (*Potentilla fruticosa* cultivars). They come in various blossom colours and they bloom all summer. The hardy 'Explorer' series and 'Parkland' series roses also bloom all summer, but may be too low for your needs. For blossoms in April, try *Forsythia* 'Northern Gold' or for blossoms in late May, try the little leaf lilac (*Syringa meyeri* 'Palibin'). For a dry sunny site, the pygmy caragana (*Caragana pygmaea*) is wonderful; for excellent fall colour, the Amur maple would work (*Acer ginnala*).

Prairie joy rose is a new, hardy, hedge rose which can be mowed to the ground each year and will still reach a 60 centimetre height during the summer.

How old does a pineapple plant have to be before it flowers and fruits?

Two to three years old. Ethylene gas brings on flowers in members of the bromeliad family such as pineapple so you may want to place a plastic bag around the mature plant with a whole apple in the bag for two weeks. This stimulates blooms and subsequent fruit. This only works, of course, where the plant is mature, so try again next spring when the plant is larger if it doesn't work this year. Do not move the plant into a bigger pot in the interim, as being pot-bound may also encourage blossoming. They do require very bright light to flower so they will benefit from being acclimated to the outdoor garden (gradually moving them into full sun) in the summer. A dilute balanced fertilizer two to three times a month in the summer is also beneficial, with additional misting of the leaves during the times when you do not fertilize. While it is important to have high humidity around the leaves and some sitting water may even be left in the leaf bases, it is important to let the soil dry out in the pot between watering.

If you are interested in starting a new plant from a pineapple fruit, first choose a fruit with healthy looking top leaves (no brown, loose, or dried portions). Twisting rather than cutting the top leaves away from the pineapple fruit will result in a small clump of fruit being pulled up. Cut this extra fruit off so the base clump of leaves is flat. Make sure to remove the lowest leaves on the clump by pulling them straight down. Removing one quarter of the leaves will result in a ring of leaf bases with a tuft of leaves above. After leaving the pineapple top on the counter for an afternoon or evening so that the cut bases dry slightly (about four hours), plant the whole thing in good potting soil up to the base of the leaves. Make sure not to fertilize until new leaves appear because it is important for the new roots to form before fertilizing begins.

Pineapple plants can be grown indoors. They take two to three years to bloom and fruit.

37

I run a coffee shop and have been wondering if I can offer coffee grinds to my customers for their compost. Will it work or is it better to throw the old grinds away?

Coffee grinds are excellent for the compost pile. They are rich in colour, and high in nitrogen and some trace elements. Go ahead and give it a try. Make sure to add other drier materials to your compost pile such as dry leaves or coarsley chopped perennials to allow oxygen to enter into the pile.

As a special treat for a friend's birthday, I want to add flowers to a salad I am making her this week. What is available this time of year that will work?

Why not purchase a single rose in her favourite colour and use it in the salad? Roses are plentiful in February and have a light, perfumed flavour. Soak the rose flower in tepid water for half an hour or so and then submerge the intact flower, with the stem removed, in a bowl of water in the fridge. Just before serving, break the petals apart and sprinkle over the salad. Use a variety of lettuce types, but concentrate on the soft butter lettuce because it will match the rose texture.

Why not crystallize a few African violet flowers for decoration as well? Using a fine paint brush, paint both petal sides of cleaned, dried African violet flowers with slightly beaten egg white and then sprinkle with berry sugar. Let dry in a cool place until the sugar has hardened.

African violet flowers make nice cake decorations.

I have seen bird mixes with the seed called "Niger thistle". Is this seed going to grow like a thistle and spread via bird feeders to become a weed like the other thistles? If so, I want to make sure it is not available in mixes anymore.

You are smart to be skeptical of bird seed mixes, but the plant you are referring to is also called Niger seed and it is not a problem flower. It is in the daisy family of plants (*Asteraceae*) and is native to Ethiopia where it grows as an annual. The Latin name is *Guizotina abyssinica* and it really is a wonderful seed for birds, especially goldfinches. I had been told it would not grow in Calgary because sellers of the seed have noticed there are never any seedlings beneath the feeders. They felt this meant it wasn't hardy and wouldn't grow. So, I tried it myself. I presoaked the seed in early May and set it in a shallow row in the garden. It germinated and quickly grew into 30-45 centimetres tall plants with yellow calendula-like blossoms at the very end of summer. Because the flowers were so late and so few, I decided I would need to start it in the house as a bedding plant if I was going to successfully raise my own Niger seed.

Goldfinches enjoy both Niger and sunflower seeds.

Niger appears to be a very long season plant and because of its habit of being an annual, I doubt it would ever become a problem on the prairies. It has become a naturalized weed in California, though, so it is worth watching. In the meantime, I will continue to feed it to the chickadees and goldfinches who visit my feeder faithfully for this high protein, high fat seed.

Can I plant tulips and hyacinths outside after they have already bloomed indoors?

Yes, but don't be surprised if it takes a few years for the tulips to rebloom and if the hyacinths die. Hyacinths are only semi-hardy in our climate; very few ever regrow and even fewer rebloom. Both tulips and hyacinths need to be allowed to gradually die back in the pot when they are finished blooming. Gradually reduce the water and then put the whole pot in the garage or basement. In late August, replant the bulbs outdoors in the garden. If the leaves are very late to bloom and to die back, you may plunk the whole thing, soil and bulb, outside in the spring in an area where they can be left undisturbed for several years.

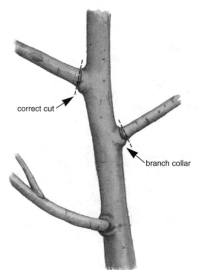

correct cut

branch collar

Proper pruning retains the branch collar.

Collar is
variable on
Poplars

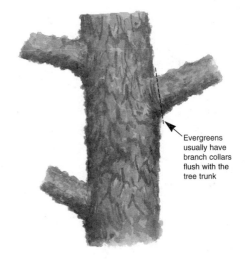

Evergreens
usually have
branch collars
flush with the
tree trunk

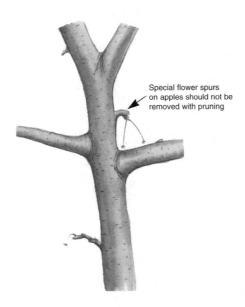

Special flower spurs
on apples should not be
removed with pruning

*Different trees have differ-
ent branch collars. Poplar,
Populus species (top),
Spruce, Picea species
(right), Apple, Malus
species (bottom).*

41

Chapter Three
M · A · R · C · H
The Great Thaw

$\mathcal{Y}$ou can almost taste it now. The air smells like spring. Seedlings are sprouting and needing transplanting; early bulbs and perennials are popping leaves out of the ground. The season for gardening is just around the corner. Worst feature of the month? Garbage starts to appear from under melting snow, and it is often half frozen and impossible to remove. It's a time for patience.

This month is full of talk of herbs, and grow lights, and the tail end of house plant questions. The potatoes are sprouting in the cool room and the grocery store, and our thoughts are turning to tree care.

March is as much about anticipation as about actual gardening. The earliest perennials and bulbs are blooming. Look for snow-drops (*Galanthus nivalis*), Dutch crocus (*Crocus* cultivars) and hepatica (*Hepatica* species) in bloom at the tail end of the month. It is a time to finish the planning and get down to work on the doing. Enjoy!

The catalogues have arrived and I'm planning to order peas and carrots, but there are so many kinds. Where do I start to get sweet, quick growing varieties for my garden?

I absolutely love all the 'Nantes' types of carrots. They are round-tipped instead of long and pointy, so are easy to pull out of the garden. They are very sweet and small cored; they are the tastiest carrots you are likely to ever grow. Some examples from the Stokes Catalogue[3] include 'Earlibird Nantes' (50 days to maturity), 'Narova' (with extra vitamins and extra sugar), and 'Spartan Premium'. The 'Imperator' style carrot is used more in the processing and commercial carrot production because they store longer and produce a very tough, easily handled carrot. These are the carrots you are likely to buy this time of year in the grocery stores, but are not advised for the home garden due to their lack of flavour.

3. Stokes Catalogue, 1994, pages 17-19. See Appendix for address.

Squill, Scilla sibirica (left).

To Do This Month:
- *Start later annuals like snapdragons, nemesia, zinnia, and petunias.*
- *Start paste tomatoes and other tomatoes from seed.*
- *Transplant, transplant, transplant. Various annuals will be sprouting, and many will need transplanting into larger seedling flats and small pots.*
- *Finish small pruning jobs as the weather warms but before the buds swell.*
- *Consider spraying with dormant oil if aphids were a problem on your trees last year.*
- *Start looking for spider mites on your houseplants. They will be waking up from their winter dormancy and may appear to come from nowhere.*

The 'Nantes' carrots (middle) are easy to pull out and full of flavor.

For years I judged agricultural fairs, and I usually tried to find the winning contestants to ask them what type of pea they were growing because I regularly saw long, straight, small but even fruited peas lined out on the plates. These peas were not just perfect in looks, they tasted great, too. I found the winners usually grew 'Green Arrow' peas and I became a convert. I also like to have some of the edible pod peas so I usually grow a row of 'Sugar Ann' which are edible at any stage and don't need staking. The pods are fat and sweet and may be stir-fried or eaten raw.

The lowest branches of my evergreens and some of the junipers are turning black and gunky. The black stuff on the stems looks like tar. What is it and what should be done about it?

It sounds like a classic example of snow mould on conifers. This disease is caused by two fungi[4], which are found naturally on the prairies. These fungi occur most frequently at higher elevations, or where branches have been buried under the snow. The main evergreens affected include alpine fir (*Abies*

4. Snow Mould on Conifers , Page 5, Forest Tree Diseases of the Prairie Provinces, Y. Hiratsuka, Information Report NOR-X-286, Northern Forestry Centre, Canadian Forestry Service, 1987.

lasiocarpa), white spruce (*Picea glauca*), Engelman spruce (*Picea engelmannii*), several species of juniper (*Juniperus* species), lodgepole pine (*Pinus contorta var. latifolia*), and limber pine (*Pinus flexilis*). Brown to black felt-like mats are seen on the lower branches. Only the affected needles and branches will die so this disease is not a big problem on larger trees, but may effectively kill low growing junipers or small seedling pines and spruce. There is no practical control recommended but rest assured it will not kill a mature tree.

When should I wrap the base of my birch tree (*Betula* species) to prevent the birch leafminer from crawling back up in spring?

Birch leafminers are actually the legless larvae of a small flying insect called a sawfly. They survive over winter as larvae in the soil or in leaf litter, pupate in the spring, and then fly as adults to find a mate and lay eggs in the fresh new birch leaves. In other words, wrapping the bark of the trunk would have absolutely no effect on the activities of these insects. This

Snow mould looks like tar but is not a problem for mature trees.

question helps to point out why it is so important to understand an insect's life cycle before trying to determine how to control it. In the case of birch leafminer, soil-applied systemic chemicals are usually recommended. They are most effective if used early, just as soon as the leaves on the trees are fully open and then repeated once more in early summer. This insect (which is actually three different species) will not kill the tree, but is usually a sign of tree stress. It occurs on virtually every city-grown tree, especially those birch of introduced rather than native sources. The native North American birches, when watered properly, suffer less from leafminer attacks than the introduced European birch trees.

Birches rarely get the moisture they need and are therefore prone to stress. If you promote tree health by mulching the base of the tree with 10-15 centimetres of organic material such as bark chips; avoid cultivating the soil around the tree; avoid planting flowers at the tree base (which disturbs the roots); and make sure to water frequently; the tree will be healthier and will be able to survive an occasional attack of leafminers. One final note regarding birch trees: they do not like to be pruned at all, but especially if the branches are wider than two centimetres in diameter. At least one reference suggests pruning may even attract additional attention from insects, which is a good reason to keep all pruning, not just on birch trees, but all woody plants, to a minimum.

I am interested in information about creating, planting, and caring for a lily pond or outdoor pool. Would the pond be affected if it is in a different climate such as Vegreville, Alberta?

This is a very big request, so I will suggest a simple starting point, and as your skills improve, you may wish to develop a more detailed lily pond. Start with a prefabricated fibreglass pool. Dig a hole in the garden to accommodate the size and depth of the pool. For a more natural effect, place the pool a bit deeper than the surrounding soil, and add rock on the pool's edge to overlap the edge of the fibreglass. Then use plants around the edge of the pool such as marsh marigold (*Caltha palustris*), flowering rush (*Butumus umbellatus*), Siberian iris or even native bulrushes from a nearby marsh. A new dwarf bulrush (*Typha minima*) is very nice near a small creek or pond.

Place the waterlilies in pots in the pond rather than trying to plant them directly in the pond. For best success, install a self-contained pump to keep the water moving and splashing. If the pond is in a shady area, the addition of native ferns by the water's edge will also accent the natural look. Additionally, colewort (*Crambe cordifolia*) will add a coarse textured look.

Your garden's location in Vegreville will not affect your success with this simple project. People often do fail with cement based ponds because they crack in the freezing and thawing cycle of our falls, winters, and springs. Another alternative is a pool liner of rubber or plastic sheeting. These will not crack from freezing and thawing but may be accidentally pierced. A nice combination is to overlay the natural looking free-form flexible

Waterlilies (above) are best planted in pots rather than directly into the bottom of the pond.

Instead of spraying with growth regulators to control the height of bedding plants, growers are finding that touching them is doing the same thing. To keep bedding and other indoor plants short and compact, touch them every day or place a light piece of plexiglass over the tray of seedlings for a few moments each day to get the same effect.

If you can keep the early morning temperatures cooler than the evening temperatures, your plants will also be stockier. This differs from our normal household practise of keeping the temperature cool at night and warm during the day.

liner with a concrete base. In this case, if the cement cracks, the flexible liner will hold the water. Natural rocks may then be cemented around the edges of the stream and pond. Several companies such as Lee Valley Tools now sell "Pool kits". Moores Water Gardens are a good source of outdoor pool plants.

Help! My bulbs are starting to come up. Should I water them?

No! Believe it or not, bulb leaves have a telescoping lifestyle. They will come up and go back down as the temperatures rise and fall. If you water them now, they will come up too far and will not be able to retract back down if the weather cools again. So, instead, throw a little leftover snow over them, or cover the beds with a few evergreen branches (from your Christmas tree?) to keep them cooler, more shady, and less likely to bloom prematurely.

How do you get a jade plant to bloom?

It is partially a function of age. Mature jade plants bloom every winter or early spring. Reduce the water slightly in the late fall. Then when you start watering normally again in January or February, the plant will burst into bloom if the light levels are bright enough.

My carrots all had extensive tunnelling and a small, rusty headed, worm-like insect in them last fall. What happened and how do I prevent it this spring?

Is there an organic way to get rid of carrot fly?

From the description of the damage mentioned in the first question, I suspect you have carrot rust fly. The best answer for carrot rust fly (referred to as carrot fly in the second question) is prevention so I am answering both questions together.

Adult rust flies emerge from the garden soil in the spring, and perhaps again later in the summer, depending on the number of generations per year in your area. Some authors suggest they lay their eggs directly in the crown of the young plant while others suggest eggs are laid in the soil near plants. Studies are still underway to see how many generations there are per year in northern gardens.

In the greatly extended British Columbia bug season, there are at least two or three generations of rust flies per summer so, depending on the generation, the eggs are laid either in the bare spring soil or at the base of the plant. In other regions, we don't know for sure yet if we have a single generation or two. Regardless, the adult carrot rust fly is easily recognized: it is a small, black fly with yellowish legs and a yellow-brown head. The wings are distinctively attached very low on the fly's middle body part. Like many insects, they are attracted to

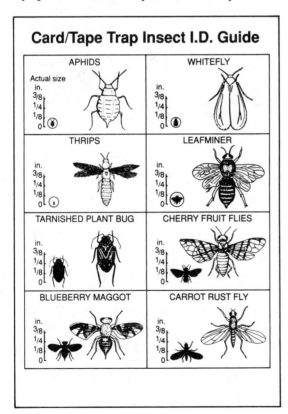

CHART USED WITH PERMISSION OF PHERO TECH INC.

Recognizing an insect is half the battle. Use this chart to identify carrot rust fly and other common garden pests.

49

yellow sticky surfaces (the yellow emits an ultraviolet pattern which attracts insects). You could hang yellow sticky cards a few inches above your row of carrots and check them weekly for adults.[5]

Adult rust flies lay their eggs in the soil where they smell carrot seeds. Your first line of defence is to seed the carrots in a new location where there is less chance of adult flies emerging. Next, try adding one centimetre of sand over the seed when you sow it. The new location will prevent the overwintering pupae from emerging as adults right where the new seed is placed. The sand over the row of seeded carrots will prevent the emerging flies from recognising the new carrot site.

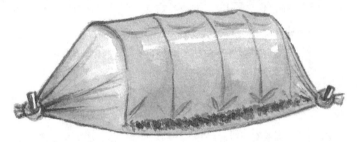

An alternative to the sand is a row covering such as Reemay, a polyester fabric much like interfacing. This cloth is laid over the row of carrots and held in place with soil or rocks placed along the fabric edges. Reemay will prevent the adult rust flies from laying their eggs among the germinating carrot seeds. The floating row cover may have to be left on the carrots until late July or August, depending on the number of generations in your area. Under the Reemay, or even a very fine tent of fine nylon, the carrots will continue to develop normally and free of invaders. Floating row covers are available from specialty garden shops including Lee Valley Tools which sells mail-order across Canada (see appendix), while tents may be built as small

Reemay cloth is an effective barrier against egg-laying carrot rust flies.

5. Yellow Sticky tags are available from many biological control suppliers including Phero Tech Inc. See Appendix.

triangular frames with the mesh stapled to the frame. These tents may be built in sections to cover raised beds entirely or in long narrow frames to cover rows of plants. A similar system may also be useful for controlling insects on all the cole crops including broccoli, kale, cabbage, and cauliflower to "exclude" cabbage loopers.

Simply finding a new location for the carrots is not enough. Once the carrot rust fly is in your neighbourhood, it will be on the lookout for carrots, parsnips, celery, or parsley seeded in the garden. The new carrot cultivar - 'Fly Away F1 Hybrid' - was reported to be resistant to rust flies. It was introduced by Thompson & Morgan in 1994 and is low in chlorogenic acid which is necessary for the larvae of the rust fly to develop. When it was trialed in a home garden in 1994, it was a disaster - bad tasting and full of carrot rust fly tunnels! Back to the drawing board.

We had slugs attacking our Norland (red) potatoes last year while our white potatoes which were nearby were untouched. Why is that?

Maybe you've discovered something new? Perhaps the white potatoes are more resistant to slug attacks because of their tougher skins. On the other hand, they may have been hilled a little more or located in a slightly drier part of the garden which is less likely to attract slugs. Switch their locations next year and see if it makes any difference. Details on general defence against slugs start in the July section.

Can one prune a mugo pine (*Pinus mugo*) to make it dense and compact after it has been left neglected and reached two or three metres tall with very bare lower branches?

No, it is not advised. Mugos grow by sending a single flush of growth out each year. They rarely sprout from lower branches and always shed needles that are older than five to seven years. This means older branches will be bare of needles. Most

Broccoli is a great vegetable in the garden but, after months of growing and caring for it, most people only eat a small part (the flower buds) and the rest of the plant is usually tossed. Gardeners who use Reemay screening to cover their veggies won't have to worry about chemicals in the leaves so they can "branch out" and eat more than just the broccoli flowers. The entire stem may be peeled and eaten. Even the leaves may be steamed or stir fried (they taste like spicy collards) instead of throwing them away.

people prune their mugos annually to prevent this legginess. With all this said, it may still be worth attempting a reduction on one or two of the main branches just to see if you can coax new growth. The tree may have to be removed from the spot anyway, so it isn't a great loss if it doesn't work. (See February for diagram.)

Who is a supplier of good topsoil?

Depending on where you live there will be sources of good soil aplenty, or only the scantest resources available. Prairie soils are generally good, but in the Luvisolic soil regions of the forested areas in the northern half of the provinces or in the mountains, there is less chance of getting unmodified soil that meets your expectations. Often local landscapers are able to use plentiful natural resources to improve or increase the bulk of soils found in the area. By adding quantities of peat moss, spent mushroom compost, or aged farmyard manure, soils may be improved or quantities enlarged before they are sold. If possible, have a look at the pile of soil available before you place your order. Be especially watchful for weeds and clumps of quack grass roots which are very obvious in unscreened or unimproved soils. Also, look for signs of white on the surface of stockpiled soils. Some areas are naturally high in alkaline and this will be noticeable as white crusting on the soil surface. Ask for soil test results.

Finally, feel the soil yourself. Work it in your hands to see that it is neither too sticky or too fine and dusty. A good soil will hold together in a ball shape for a moment after it is squeezed in your hand as long as it is moist when you do this hand texture test. Soils with high clay will keep the ball shape and not collapse back when prodded while highly sandy soils may not clump together at all.

What is the recommended height for grow lights used for seedlings and geranium cuttings?

To find out what type of soil you have, fill a jar with 2/3 topsoil and 1/3 water. Swirl and shake the slurry well and let stand for a few days. The sand will settle to the bottom, then silt, then clay. Organic matter will rise to the top. A good garden loam has 40% sand, 40% silt, and 20% clay. Does yours make the grade?

Ideally, the fluorescent tubes will not be covered with a plastic shield. The bare bulbs are perfect 15-20 centimetres above the tops of young seedlings or cuttings. To get them at this ideal distance either have the lights on chains which may be raised or lowered to suit the crop and its growth or have the plants on movable shelves. Gradually raise the lights or lower the shelves as the young seedlings grow. Each time the distance beyond 15 centimetres doubles, the light levels are decreased drastically and are far less than half the light intensity.

Young seedlings do not require full spectrum or warm lights. They thrive just fine on ordinary cool tubes because only the blue portion of the light spectrum is needed to produce leafy growth. Geraniums will need the full range of light (warm lights) to trigger bloom.

Stands with moveable shelves and/or lights provide flexibility as the seedlings grow.

My potatoes are already sprouting. Can they be given to a neighbour to use in his garden this spring?

Probably not, because ideally potatoes aren't planted outdoors until late May or early June. They are a warm season crop. The only way to keep them a bit longer would be to cool down their storage spot considerably, or plant them indoors in a barrel or large pot before the outdoor temperatures warm the soil. With all the potato diseases including bacterial, fungal, and viral, I usually recommend people buy fresh, certified disease-free stock each spring anyway, so in your case I would recommend the compost pile for your taters.

Is it OK to put ashes from the fireplace in the garden?

Can we place ashes from our fireplace in our garden or compost pile?

Yes. Wood ash may be saved and added as-is to the compost. On average, wood ash contains 1% phosphorus, 25% calcium, and 5-10% potash (potassium). It also discourages slugs when scattered around young plants because it is gritty. In other words, you may want to hang on to fireplace/wood ash and store it for spring use around your bedding plants and seedlings.

Some people worry about the high pH of wood ash, but if peat moss or compost is also added to the soil regularly, the two will balance each other. Because the application of wood ash at a rate of 20 pounds per 1000 square foot will be the same as adding six pounds of lime which would raise the pH one point, limit the applications to what you have available from your own fireplace and don't go looking for outside sources. Coal or coal ash are not recommended.

What herbs can be grown indoors at this time of year?

Many herbs appreciate being started indoors at this time of

A really unusual use of wood ash comes from the Phillipines: "Preserve only newly picked tomatoes which are ripe but not soft and overripe. Select a wooden or cardboard box and line it with paper. Gather cool ash from the cooking fire and sift to remove sharp particles. Spread the ash on the bottom, 1.5 inches thick. Arrange the tomatoes upside down in one layer and pour another thin layer of ash on top. Add another layer of tomatoes, etc. Cover and seal the container. You can extend the season in which tomatoes are available for three months."[6]

---

6. The Avant Gardener, page 9 Vol. 24, No 2. Tomatoes in Ashes, 1993.

year. Start with the ones you are likely to use in your favourite recipes. My personal favourites are basil, parsley, oregano, rosemary, and thyme. I also use very small quantities of sage and tarragon. Rosemary is a woody shrub which takes several days or even weeks to germinate. Once it is up and transplanted into a pot, leave it undisturbed in that pot for years. I put mine out in the spring and bring it back inside in the fall. Over 50 kinds of basil, which is an annual, were tested at the Brooks research station in the early 1990's. There are licorice, lemon, mint, and traditional flavours of basil. It is a very variable plant both in flavour and form. The miniature spicy-globe varieties are well suited to indoor culture if they can be kept warm and well lit under artificial lights. Parsley is a biennial but may be grown indoors for instant picking as required. Thyme, oregano, and tarragon are very hardy and are well suited to being moved outdoors once the weather stabilizes. Sage is somewhat hardy. If it doesn't overwinter for you, start it again next spring.

Should iris bloom in the first year from a tuber?

It depends on how large the tuber was last fall and what kind of condition it was in when it was purchased and planted. If it was allowed to shrivel and dry before you received it, or if it is a very small portion of tuber, it may be struggling just to make it through the winter. Different kinds of iris also have different sized tubers. The miniature, early blooming dwarf iris cultivars may bloom easily in the first year. The gigantic, larger iris which reach a height of up to a metre or more will need a few years to bloom from planting. Make sure the tubers are exposed this spring and not buried by fall blown debris or soil. A site with excellent drainage and a slight slope is best.

Cilantro is an unusual herb first introduced to me by my sister Delima when she returned from Greece with a delectable lemon soup recipe which required cilantro. Since then, I've discovered it is easily started outdoors directly from seed which may be purchased as coriander from any bulk spice store. The summer harvested leaves are called cilantro and they are excellent in all kinds of dishes including fresh tomato salsa. In the fall, if we get a really long season, the "coriander" seeds may be harvested and either ground for use in East Indian dishes or saved for spring planting.

Chapter Four

A · P · R · I · L

Tasks At Hand

$\mathcal{T}$he lawns are thawed and the soil is warming; the smell of denitrifying bacteria is in the air. Yuck! The earliest garden centres are opening with teaser specials; peat moss is a deep discount item aimed at luring you to the greenhouse or nursery; and the earliest perennials, especially the alpines, are beginning to bloom in the garden.

Be the first on your block to spot an early beacon of spring, the mourning cloak butterfly. Start the later annual flowers, and put the brakes on pruning. The flower buds and some leaf buds may be emerging this month on trees and shrubs, so pruning is now a no-no. Instead, try some gentle raking of debris from under and around your perennials and shrubs. Toss these rakings into the compost pile. Also, direct seed some of the earliest annual flowers in the garden by mid-April when the soil is still cool.

This is the gearing up season for gardening, and it inspires the keen at heart and even the diffident to "do something". Maybe it's the long winter that inspires us, or maybe it's some primeval urge to plant the crops and till the soil. Either way, don't resist the urge to get your hands dirty this month but do resist the urge to fertilize lawns. Wait until at least Mother's Day for lawn fertilizing. 🍃

What types of grass are good to grow in the shade close to the house with lots of animal interference? When should I plant it? Or, what type of shrubbery would work in the same spot?

You may be overly optimistic to find a single solution to landscaping an area as troublesome as this spot close to the house with shade **and** animal interference! If the area is too shady or the animals too aggressive, you may be better off placing a mulch over the soil nearest the house. Depending on the house colour you may choose a fine gravel, or even an organic bark mulch or layer of woodchips. In front of that, any shade

Drumstick primula (Primula denticulata) with a mourning cloak butterfly (left).

To Do This Month:
🍃 *Spray dormant oils where aphids and spider mites were a problem last summer.*
🍃 *Seed late annuals like marigolds, cosmos, and broccoli indoors.*
🍃 *Direct seed earliest cool season annuals outdoors including annual larkspur, sunflower, lavatera, bachelor's buttons, clary sage, or poppies.*
🍃 *Transplant the earlier started seedlings into flats or bigger pots.*

Shady areas require special considerations. Ostrich fern, <u>Anemone sylvestris,</u> and <u>Hosta</u> make a great trio of hardy perennials in the shade garden.

loving plant or group of plants would work.

Avoid leggy or fragile plants such as bleeding heart (*Dicentra* species) or ostrich ferns (*Matteuccia struthiopteris*) because they won't stand up to animal interference. Try instead the very coarse and sturdy hostas (*Hosta* species), lily-of-the-valley (*Convallaria majalis*), or goutweed (*Aegopodium podagraria*). Further away from the home, say about six feet, try shade tolerant shrubs like dogwood (*Cornus* species).

Beyond the mulches, groundcovers, and shrubs you may want to introduce grass, but because of the low light, I would recommend a grass mixture including fescues and bluegrass. Individual grasses in the mixture will develop or die out as the grass establishes. These mixes are widely available at garden centres and farm supply centres.

I would like to know about Canadian mosses or liverworts. Are there any good books on this subject?

Yes, a book published by Lone Pine Press entitled "Mosses,

Lichens, and Ferns of Northwest North America" includes colour photos on every page and should answer every question you've ever had on this topic.

Do tomatoes grow well in Calgary?

Is this a trick question? By grow well do you mean bloom, produce fruit, **and** ripen fruit on the vine in lush quantities? Calgary's altitude of 3200 feet means we have colder nights than Edmonton or even Grande Prairie in the summer, and it is only technically possible to grow tomatoes here. They need a lot of extra care if you expect them to "thrive", and you need to be careful to select very short season plants which, coincidentally, also usually have very small fruit.

I have drifted over the years towards Roma or Italian style tomatoes. I prefer these because they are very heavy producers which set fruit in our cool evenings without special care or sprays. Then they go on to produce heavy crops of three or more kilograms of fruit per plant. The fruit doesn't always ripen on the vine, but it is very dry by nature and it will continue to gradually ripen in the house until late into November. This means you could have fresh tomatoes for use in stews, soups, or sauces long after the growers of large "juicy" tomatoes are through eating their entire harvest. Paste tomatoes are very thick walled, meaty, and sweet.

I start tomatoes from seed in early March or early April under lights and move them outdoors under hot caps or in the protection of the house once the evenings warm slightly. I have been caught with June 23rd and August 8th frosts in the same season, which was a disaster, but that was only one season out of the past sixteen. I'm usually successful, and you should be too if you adjust your sights and extend the season by using protective covers in the spring.

Use a fertilizer with balanced numbers to ensure your plants are getting the potassium they need to make the best possible use of

Warm your garden soil in the spring by moistening it and then covering it with clear plastic for one or two weeks. This will also trigger germination of weed seeds which can then be pulled before your crop is grown. Another way to have warmer soil in the spring is to build raised beds for your vegetables. Soils are always cooler when they are dry, so if nothing else, water the soil in the spring prior to planting if you have experienced a long dry spell.

Larger tomatoes must be staked properly to allow maximum growth.

"Tomato seedlings are best planted out in the mid-afternoon", says the University of California. "Seedlings set out on cold mornings are more susceptible to chilling injury because their metabolic reserves have been depleted during the night."[7]

the nitrogen and phosphorus in the fertilizer and in the soil. If you have a sheltered south facing spot near your home, this will give your tomatoes an added edge.

Larger fruited types of tomatoes such as 'Ultra Girl' will require staking and pruning to be successful in cool climates. Prune out all side branches and allow only a single stalk to form. Use rebar or old hockey sticks as stakes but make sure the stakes are at least two metres tall because you will need this height in really warm seasons. Tie the tomato stalks to the stakes with old nylons or pantyhose which are looped around the tomato stem in a figure-eight fashion so they will not restrict the growth of the plant. Old soft cloths may be as good as nylons, but most other ties are too firm and you risk damage to the tomato stem in windy weather.

Ideally, move the location of your tomato plants each year on a three to five year rotation plan with other vegetables.

I am looking for a herb called "Rue". I was told it grows here.

Rue (*Ruta graveolens*) is an old-fashioned herb well known for its distinctive scent which is musky and certainly not loved by all. Expect this perennial to grow to a height of 30-60 centimetres with finely divided grey-green leaves. Like most grey-leaved plants, Rue prefers full sun; it also appears to be an insect repellent. While some people use it medicinally, it is known to be toxic to some people so it should not be used internally. Look for it with the perennial plants at your favorite garden centre instead of with the other herbs.

What is the best way to get plants growing on a slope? I want to prevent the soil from washing off in the recent spring showers and I am anxious to have the area green.

Use a fabric (not plastic) weed barrier around the plantings on a slope and top this off with a heavy layer of at least

---

7. The Avant Gardener, Pg 40, Vol. 25, No 5. March 1993.

15 centimetres of mulch to hold the barrier in place. If the slope is very extreme, you may have to terrace it in layers slightly first, and then place the plants and fabric. A slow trickle of water, or a drip system, will ensure good moisture without runoff in the earliest stages of establishment. A large rock or two on the lower side of each shrub on the slope will slow down the movement of water as it passes by the shrub.

Slopes are ideal for all kinds of woody plants because they guarantee there will never be water sitting and soaking the crown of the plant; this means the roots will never suffer from a lack of oxygen which is common in waterlogged soils. The best trees and shrubs for a slope, especially a slope on a large property, are those with spreading or suckering characteristics, especially those plants that can tolerate some drought. Try wolf willow (*Elaeagnus commutata*), native willows of all kinds (*Salix* species), or horizontal junipers (*Juniperus horizontalis*). Groundcovers such as periwinkle (*Vinca minor*) and cliff green (*Paxistima canbyi*) are also excellent.

Tufted grasses like blue fescue (*Festuca glauca*) and blue oat grass (*Helictotrichon sempervirens*) as well as tough perennials like prairie coneflower (*Ratibida columnifera*), purple coneflower (*Echinaceae purpurea*), blue flax (*Linum perenne*), and baby's breath (*Gypsophila paniculata*) also work smartly on slopes. I have seen people lay burlap over freshly seeded perennial flowers to keep them shaded and moist until they germinate on slopes. It is very important, though, that the burlap cover come off as soon as the seedlings germinate or they will grow right through the fabric and get pulled out, roots and all, when the burlap is removed later.

What is the best way to plant a rose?

On a slant if the roots are grafted and there are more roots than you can accommodate in the top 45 centimetres of soil, or straight up if the rose is on its own roots or if the roots are severely amputated.[8]

The reasoning here is that grafted roses (most hybrids and many of our shrub roses - ask the supplier) are very tender at the graft point and they need to have a ten centimetre soil cover above this point.

Healthy, vigorously-rooted roses (especially those on their own roots) are best planted the same way as all other shrubs - straight up and down. If there isn't enough room in the prepared hole to accommodate the rose roots in the top 15-30 centimetres of soil, the shrub may go in on a slant. Remember, if the rose is grafted, and it dies above the graft, it may sucker from below the graft which will produce an entirely different rose than planted. So, look over your site, consider the rose and its roots, and then decide on the planting style.

The slant technique of planting roses is preferred by many growers for grafted roses, because it helps protect the graft zone and encourages rooting of the rose above the graft. This technique involves laying the rose at a 45 degree angle in a 45 centimetre deep prepared soil trench so that the graft point (which is the obvious lump on the stem) is ten centimetres below the soil surface. The roots will all be in the top 15-30 centimetre layer of soil. The soil above the graft must be loose and coarse with plenty of grit and sand. This allows additional rooting and sprouting of the rose above the graft point which is desirable.

Protect the top growth of newly planted roses with damp burlap or newspaper for up to a week to prevent moisture loss through the softened stems. Another idea is to place a plant pot around the new rose with the bottom of the pot cut away so that there is some wind and sun shelter for the first few days after planting.

---

8. Page 34, Rose Gardening on the Prairies, George Shewchuck. Book strongly discourages buying roses on poor, amputated root stocks. The relative success with roses relies on the original healthy roots.

Ideal planting time is as early as the soil can be worked and before the rose has leafed out.

Many mail-order roses come in damp newspaper and may have dried out somewhat in shipping. If they seem a bit dry, revive them by plunging the roots of the rose into a bucket of water mixed with a handful of soil. The rose may be left in this muddy slurry for an hour or several before planting but should not be left like this overnight or longer.

Are juniper berries (*Juniperus* species) poisonous?

No. They are certainly enjoyed by fall and winter foraging birds, especially grosbeaks. Juniper "berries" which are actually a special type of cone, closer in their role to a pine cone than true berry, are used as flavouring in gin. They are astringent and don't really taste that great, but the birds love them and eat them heartily in mid-winter when their other resources are running low.

There is a seed pod on my African violet plant. I have never seen this before. Is it rare?

Yes, it is rare to have a seed pod on an African violet. The pollen must have been transferred from one flower to the next. Did you do it yourself with a paintbrush, or did a fly or bee do it for you? The pollen may have even been transferred accidentally if the plant was knocked slightly. The seeds should be easy to start in a warm, moist soil. Give it a try, but remember to expect the unexpected. Hybrid seed may not grow, and if it does, the young seedling and the flowers they later produce will all be different from the mother plant.

I have a peony in a shady spot and would like to move it to a sunnier spot? Can it be moved now?

If you can possibly leave the peony in this spot until fall, do that. This is not the ideal time to move a peony. It sounds like your plant is in a less than ideal spot, though, because peonies

Think carefully about where to plant a peony. It is truly a 'no sweat' plant in the right conditions. Paeonia cultivars include many different flower types.

do prefer full sun to partial shade. If you do decide to move it, do it right away, or at least before it is more than 15 centimetres above ground.

How do you transplant a peony?

In the fall, preferably only every 40 years. Wait until the growth has started to die back in the fall, then gently dig the plant and either cut apart or gently tug the roots to separate them. You will notice tiny pink buds on the roots which resemble the "eyes" of potatoes. It is critical to replant the peony so these eyes are exactly the same level below the soil as they were before. They cannot tolerate being deeper than four centimetres below the soil and prefer to be in the top two to four centimetres. When peonies fail to bloom, it is usually because the plant was put in too deep. They are very finicky about depth. Make sure there are five "eyes" on each piece. Peonies are the plant that gave perennials a good name. They never get invasive or outgrow their spot and they really don't need transplanting for at least a generation or two. Most people only move them if they are in the way of construction or if a friend wants a piece.

Help! My weeping birch (*Betula pendula*) is being attacked by aphids. Would Tanglefoot work?

No. Tanglefoot is a sticky glue-like product which traps insects because they stick to it as they try to crawl their way up a tree trunk. Insects get stuck and die as they climb up the trunk. Aphids on a tree at this time of year are wingless and they most likely overwintered on the tree in the bark cracks and buds. Aphids are not tree climbers in the spring; in August, when aphids grow wings and fly away, they are still not tree climbers. In other words, there is no way that Tanglefoot will stop aphids from being high on a tree in spring.

Aphids are a sign the tree is under stress. You must have a close look at your tree care methods to determine what is causing stress in your birch. Is it competing with the lawn for moisture and nutrients? Was it planted too deep originally so that the natural flare of the tree is below the soil surface and the roots are now desperate for moisture and oxygen? Has it been pruned heavily or sprayed heavily in the past? These things may all cause stress in a tree, and may make your tree the aphid roost of the neighbourhood. It is still early in the season and a shot of mineral oil mixed with water to make up a dormant oil solution may work to suffocate the just-awakening aphids. Some experiments using soap mixed with dormant oil have been effective. Follow instructions for dormant oil application from the label on the product. Dormant oil is a light mineral oil and is sold at most garden centres.

Tanglefoot and other similar sticky products painted in a band around trees in mid-September prevents adult female fall cankerworms from climbing up the tree to lay eggs. If you have had a problem with this insect before, try this sticky solution this fall.

Is it time to fertilize our lawns yet? They are still brown, but I can see a bit of green coming through and the soil is thawed in most areas now.

No, it is still too early to fertilize. I always hold off until the soil warms and the lawn is almost green. Naturally occurring denitrifying bacteria have been producing nitrogen over the winter, and this small source of nitrogen will get the lawn through the earliest phases of spring. If you gamble and pour commercial fertilizers on the lawn too early you may get a rich thick flush of growth, but you may also get a late snowfall and that may be followed by snow mould which particularly likes cool temperatures and high nitrogen turf. Be patient.

Tell me about this term chitting? What does it mean? How do you do it?

Chitting means presoaking seeds before planting them and translates into faster sprouting once the seed is in the ground. It is an old practise, and it is smart gardening. Grandma used to soak her peas and beans overnight in a quart sealer, because she knew these seeds would sprout quicker in the garden with presoaking. Because seeds take in so much moisture before

Look for ladybeetles and their larvae in trees with aphids. The adults eat aphids whole and lay eggs which hatch into aphideating larvae.

Snow mould appears as a whitish or pinkish haze on the lawn in the spring. Brushing the visible signs of this fungus vigorously with a wisk broom will help eliminate it.

Get your veggie transplants off to an early and protected start by covering them with a mini-cloche. A what? Any covering such as a plastic tunnel may extend the season by protecting the plants at night and keeping them warmer and out of the wind during the day. Many gardeners use 4-litre milk cartons or 3-litre plastic pop containers with their bottoms cut off. Thread an old clothesline or rope through the handles of the milk cartons and hang the works out of the sun in a shed or garage once the season settles and the plants become established. These cheap cloches will last up to four seasons.

they are able to sprout, growth may be delayed until the moisture comes along to meet the seed's needs unless the seeds are chitted first.

Chitted seed sprouts right away which means earlier growth and a quicker harvest. Also, fewer seeds will rot in cool spring soil awaiting the moisture they need to push the little seed roots and leaves out into the soil and sky. Chitting seems to work with any seed including carrots and even grass. A prechitted lawn will emerge in two to three days compared with six to 20 days for unchitted seed.

Carrots will emerge almost overnight if chitted. The problem? Chitted seed will be wet and will clump together. It needs to be mixed with dry vermiculite or dry sand just prior to seeding so that it is distributed evenly and not all dumped, bean sprout style, in a clump.

What do you think of potentilla as a hedge?

I like it where a naturally shaped hedge is the goal and where the location is sunny. Potentillas stay fairly small and bloom furiously all summer, have few pests, and are completely hardy. They don't necessarily suit shearing, though, so should be planted where there is space to let them attain their natural size. Also, potentilla will not get high enough to form a two metre high barrier which is often the goal of hedge-growers.

Where do I get a compact mugo pine and, most importantly, how do I keep it that way?

Many dwarf forms of mugo pine are on the market including the compact mugo pine (*Pinus mugo* 'compacta' and *Pinus mugo* 'pumilio'). These are dwarf by nature and may be kept that way and further reduced in size by trimming the candles each spring (See diagram in February).

My Virginia creeper had sprouted early and was killed by frost. Should it be cut back now?

I always hate to second guess a woody plant. If you cut your creeper (*Parthenocissus quinquefolia*) back now, you may be cutting back the very twigs with the stored energy or dormant buds necessary to allow the plant to sprout on its own. This adds an extra stress to a plant which has already suffered a set-back. It is far better to wait and see where the plant resprouts, which it surely will do, and wait to cut out any dead or damaged branches once the vine is in full leaf and full growth in mid-June.

How large do you need to make a compost pile?

At least a cubic metre if you are trying to build an aerobic (oxygen-needing), hot pile of compost. Anything smaller probably won't ever reach the internal heat it needs to quickly decompose the materials added. Once you begin composting, chances are you'll want at least three piles of at least a cubic metre each. There will suddenly be so much more going on the pile and so little going to the dump. An average family's garbage contains 30% compostables.

If the compost bin is smaller than the minimal size, it will not heat up high enough to break the materials down quickly. They may stay in their original form for a long, impatient while. In other cases, the pile may be so huge it is impossible to turn; this leads to anaerobic rather than aerobic composting. The oxygen-poor pile will definitely stink, may attract mice, and will turn to a kind of sludge rather than nice crumbly soil. People using an entirely different method of composting, involving worms, don't need a large space, because the goal is not heat, but worm munching. This is usually carried on indoors where the worms can eat comfortably year round.

How do you rejuvenate a lawn?

Why bother? I have done this, but only once. I was sure if I tore out the old lawn and reseeded a new one, I would have a lusher more enviable green space. Following a lengthy spell to kill and remove the lawn, I then had to redo the whole thing.

I now know that improving the maintenance on an existing lawn is almost always preferable. Start this spring by mowing the lawn very short before it regrows. Then aerate and dethatch. Top up the "lawn" with one centimetre of fine screened loam raked evenly over the soil surface, and finish up with extra pre-chitted[9] lawn seed on any areas that were bare or thin last fall. Follow-up with regular watering and lawn care over the summer and your lawn will look rejuvenated without the mess of stripping out the old to put in the new.

I have a Hawaiian schefflera which is losing the lower leaves. They turn yellow and hang on for a while before they fall off.

Sounds like a classic example of low nitrogen levels. If you haven't fertilized for a while, do so now. The higher light levels in the spring often stimulate a flush of new growth on houseplants, and the plants will rob from the older leaves to give to the newer, younger growth. Use a balanced fertilizer such as 20-20-20, because if the plant is low on nitrogen it's possible it needs other nutrients as well.

What is the best way to get rid of spider mites on house plants? What type of chemical or natural soap works best?

Pure soap flakes mixed with warm water with a drop of pure vegetable oil is a dandy home remedy for mites on house plants. Mix the works together in a hand spray bottle, shaking vigorously to ensure the particles are well combined and the mixture stays in suspension while in use. Put your emphasis on the leaf undersides which is where the mites will be feeding. Follow up a week later with a soap and water solution and repeat again each week until the mites have all hatched, been sprayed, and are dead. It is common to find mites on house-plants in the spring which makes it seem that they appear "miraculously" or spontaneously. In fact, they have just gone

9. See earlier question on chitting.

dormant on the window ledges or in cracks of the plant's buds and bark. Look for them again next spring and treat as usual. Occasionally, put the entire plant in the shower with tepid water to wash off any clinging insects or soap residue. Watch for leaf edges browning or other signs of soap induced trouble. Keep from breathing in the soap solution, because it works by asphyxiating insects, so could cause trouble with your own breathing if you are not cautious.

What is a good perennial that blooms for a long time?

You haven't given many clues to suggest what your favourite colour might be or what your growing conditions are. I'm guessing you like blue flowering perennials which don't become invasive or too weedy. A very easy to grow hardy plant of this type is the blue flax (*Linum perenne*) which is about 45 centimetres tall and blooms from mid-May to late summer. Any yellow flowering annual or perennial looks smashing with this dainty plant. Flax also comes in white. An annual flax which is very similar in appearance comes in red.

What do you do about all the extra leaves hanging on a lilac (or any shrub) since last fall?

Occasionally winter comes too quick, or the shrubs in a certain setting wait too long before getting ready for it. In either case, your first hint of a problem is when the leaves fail to change colour in the fall and instead, hang on all winter. This means the energy reserves in the leaves were not fully moved into the branches and down to the roots. As a result, the corky layer between leaves and twigs was never formed. The shrub is trying to tell you it isn't ready for winter, and the end result will probably be winter kill in the form of twig death in the spring.

So, while there isn't really anything you can do about helping the tree or shrub at this point, the one cosmetic thing you can do is gently tug the dead leaves off. Once the shrub is fully leafed out in late May or early June you will see if there is any actual twig damage. Pruning at that time will be useful to remove dead stuff. If this is happening consistently in your yard, make sure to start encouraging early dormancy in the fall by decreasing the watering until the leaves start to change colour and then continuing with normal watering until the leaves are fully dropped.

Is there a special fertilizer for tuberous begonias?

No. Do not fertilize when first planted. Once the young plants are off to a good start, use a diluted rate of any complete fertilizer (all three numbers on the package). The easiest way to use a dilute rate is to cut the amount of fertilizer recommended on the package in half. Try water soluble 15-20-25 or a similar product which has a lower nitrogen content and a higher phosphorus content for compact sturdy growth.

My pine has tiny white marks on the needles. Is this normal?

There is one type of pine that has small white sap droplets which sound like your description. If you have a *Pinus aristata*, you are okay. This bristlecone pine naturally looks this way.

If you have any other pine with white dots on the needles you might have pine needle scale (*Phenacaspis pinifoliae*)[10]. These little white insects are two to three millimetres long with a yellow spot at one end. After overwintering as eggs under old "shells" of scales, the young larvae hatch in the spring. They are seen quite commonly on Scots pine as well as on both white and blue spruce. A dormant oil spray (follow label directions) in the late winter or early spring just before the tree starts growing is recommended if you can wait until then to control the problem. Washing the trees off vigorously with a strong stream of water, and maintaining the trees in top physical shape so they are resistant to this and other pests is the best immediate course of action. Removing the most infested branches is also a good idea. If you prefer to spray, you should do it before mating and

10. Diseases and Pests of Ornamental Plants, 4th Edition. Pascal P. Pirone, The Ronald Press Co., New York, pg.402.

egg laying which begins in August. Check for registered products at your garden centre or hardware store.

What kind of soil do you need to create a cactus garden?

Use ordinary potting soil and mix it half and half with washed sharp sand. After the soil is mixed, you may also want to add a handful of fine chicken grit to the surface of each pot to prevent the cactus from coming into contact with damp soil. The grit is available at feed stores and is really just finely crushed granite.

There is a mature spruce (25 feet tall) growing in my front yard. I would like to cut back the lower branches to make way for grass. When should this be done?

How can you get grass to grow under a spruce tree?

Don't do it! Certain death for trees, including evergreens is grass underfoot. Certain death for grass is the presence of a tree towering overhead. Evergreens shade out the grass, and gradually acidify the soil which makes an ideal environment for tree roots but a disaster zone for lawns. If the lower branches are really bothering you due to security concerns or the "look" of your yard, go ahead and remove those branches now, but mulch under it rather than planting grass. The tree health will not be compromised, and the look you want will be achieved.

To mulch under the spruce tree, first cut the lawn very short, then lay newspaper over the lawn and finally, cover the paper with a ten centimetre (four inch) layer of mulch. The paper and mulch will kill the lawn without damaging the tree roots. Be imaginative and use a variety of mulching materials to get the textural effect you want. Closer to the dripline of the tree, plant drought and acid tolerant perennials which can be left in place for a number of years. Snow-in-summer (*Cerastium tometosum*) gives a wonderful bright contrast to the deep green

Turfgrass can reduce the amount of tree roots in the top few inches of soil by 90%. This means more stress, slower growth, and predisposition to insect and disease problems.[11]

11. Tree Roots: "Dynamic and Delicate", Turfgrass, April/May 1994.

of evergreens and blends in well with a gravel mulch. It blooms in late spring with the brightest white flowers of any perennial.

My dropmore honeysuckle has its leaves too high. Can it be pruned to lower the leaves?

Yes, but check to make sure the buds have not swollen and the leaves have started to show through. If this has happened in your yard, leave the pruning until the leaves are fully out and growing. Then, take the oldest and tallest branches back right to the ground, removing a maximum of one third of the total top growth. By removing the oldest branches on this woody vine, you will be shortening its overall height and encouraging new sprouts from the base. These new sprouts will be shorter than the ones removed. You may also want to cut back a few of the tallest branches by pinching or pruning out the top 15-30 centimetres of growth.

I am planning to plant some junipers near my mature hawthorn tree and have heard there may be a problem. Have you heard of this?

Yes, there is a rust fungus disease (*Gymnosporangium* species) that needs both junipers and hawthorns (or other rose family

Avoid planting junipers and members of the rose family in the same yard. Disease symptoms on a hawthorn (left) differ from those on a juniper (right).

72

members such as Saskatoon) to complete its life cycle.[12] This causes weird disease symptoms on both plants. The hawthorn leaves will have horned bumpy spots, while the junipers will have asteroid-like jelly blobs along the branches. It is uglier than it is harmful, but will eventually add an additional stress to both plants and looks ugly. It's not worth the risk or hassles involved later, so I do not encourage planting these two woodies within the same yard.

Should you water trees and shrubs at this time of year? The soil is thawed and the buds are swollen. The soil is very dry.

Yes, where the soils are dry and thawed, the roots of the trees may have become active. Often, evergreens such as junipers will already be showing spurts of growth, and they will definitely be needing the moisture. The key here is in your question - there is no point watering frozen soils, only soils that have already thawed and are dry.

My cedar has sunscald. What can I do?

Are you sure the damage on your tree is from the sun? Many cedars show damage in the spring from animal urine in the winter. Be suspicious of yellow or brown patches on the lower side of a cedar. Only suspect sun damage if the shrub is facing directly south. Once you have this damage, regardless of the cause, there is nothing you can do. Try pruning out the affected leaves, and in the future try planting other small shrubs in front of the cedar to shade it from the direct sun and reflection off the snow. Junipers are a good choice in front of a cedar. With cats on leashes in some cities, now we can probably expect less damage from territory marking.

Is it okay to use old railway ties around a vegetable garden area?

12. Leaf and Berry Rusts of Saskatoons and other Rosaceous Hosts, Page 83, Forest Tree Diseases of the Prairie Provinces, Y. Hiratsuka, 1987. Information Report NOR-X-286, Northern Forest Research Centre.

No. Ties contain creosote, and soils that have been contaminated with creosote are not considered safe. Using anything with the creosote constantly leaking out of it (which is the case with railroad ties) won't be suitable for growing plants you want to eat! I have seen people plastic line their ties, but I am still not sure that is safe. There is also some question about the safety of using treated timbers as a raised garden frame. They may leach out their preservatives too.

Have you heard of the perennial sweet pea? Where can I get one?

The perennial sweet pea (*Lathyrus latifolius*) is hardy on the prairies but finicky. It is very hardy in older gardens where it is established, but that is the trick... it may be tough to establish. You can buy it both as seed and as a potted perennial. It is available from perennial wholesalers, so ask for it at your favourite garden centre and ask them to order it if they don't already have it in stock. It is really worth the effort to grow this vine because the purple flowers are long lasting and perfumed.

My geranium has red leaves. What is the problem?

Either it has had a touch of cold or is low on phosphorus. Have you been leaving it outside to harden it off? Keep it in a relatively warm area until later in May, and fertilize it now with a complete fertilizer, then again in a few weeks. Geraniums use a lot of fertilizer and the artificial soils we grow them in don't have much buffer capacity, so deficiency symptoms show up right away. One tip with pot grown plants and annuals in planters is to alternate the brand and formulation of fertilizer each time you fertilize. This way, if there are micronutrients missing, hopefully a different complete fertilizer will make up the shortfall.

Chapter Five
M · A · Y

The Race Is On

On your mark, get set, grow! It's finally spring. Planning time is over, and buying and planting time has arrived. There is a rush to do a year's work in a few short weekends, and our backs and knees may suffer but we love it.

This month, hold off on fertilizing the lawn until after Mother's Day; scour the nurseries for interesting new perennials to fit your scheme; start hardening off your annuals by placing them outdoors during the day; and be on the look-out for the expected bug of the week. Awareness will prevent disaster in the bug department. Why not start a garden calendar to record bloom dates and bug dates in your garden? A five year calendar will help you track your successes and target those flower-less loopholes which may be filled in for a full colour bloom all year. If you are missing colour in your garden at any time in May, you need more perennials.

This is a season of celebrating colour after our long-awaited dormant spell. Don't just wait for the annuals to begin blooming, actively seek out early blooming plants in your neighbourhood. I suggest primulas, bergenia, tulips, crocus, double flowering plum, crab-apples, 'Northern Gold' forsythia, creeping phlox in shades of white to brilliant pink, daffodils, mother-of-thyme, and other early blooming rock garden gems. With these early flowers, it won't seem a long wait until the annuals are prime.

Local garden centres will carry many of the earliest and best bloomers, or be more forthright and ask at homes with outstanding spring bloom (ask for the names of their early bloomers, not the bloomers themselves). This is the season when we are most desperate for colour so why deprive yourself? Don't forget the beneficial effect of trees in your yard; in the global picture, celebrate Arbor Day this year by planting a tree, or two, or three. *

My tulips are not blooming this spring, and the leaves are dying back already. Why didn't the tulips bloom?

Tulips, Tulipa (left).

To Do This Month:
* *Fertilize lawns after the leaves are fully expanded on the trees.*
* *Celebrate Arbor Day.*
* *Plant flowers in the garden.*
* *Start the pest patrol.*
* *Buy a new and unusual plant for your garden.*

Any tulips that were heated in storage before they were planted, especially tulips with double flowers, will abort their tiny over-wintering flower buds. To avoid problems, buy bulbs early in the fall from a reputable garden centre or mail order house. Make sure the tulips are not being stored in a storefront window or near heaters. Tulips wrapped in plastic are also more likely to heat up and abort their buds. Unfortunately, bulb heating and bud aborting causes invisible damage, so you will have to trust your retailer. I also like to buy premium sized bulbs if they are available. Buy from a supplier that has proven reliable in the past and then plant them as soon as they are brought home.

While it may be tempting to blame poor tulip success on dry spring soil, these conditions will usually only produce flowers that are dwarfed and stressed looking, not absent. If the flowers have been in for more than one year and the flowers are gradually getting smaller, this is an entirely different problem. Top up your tulip beds with manure or compost in the fall and remember to toss a little extra lawn fertilizer their way to add nitrogen when the tulips are a few centimetres out of the ground. Finally, let the leaves die back fully and naturally. This will help boost bulb development.

The colour yellow is hard for our eyes to process so it is not a favourite colour overall, but it has been shown to stimulate memory (hence yellow legal pads). Why not combine a few memory enhancing Primula auriculas with the non-threatening and neutral blue blooming forget-me-nots (Myosotis species) or blue flax (Linum perenne) in your spring garden?

When do you dig up tulips to put in annuals?

Try to find a spot in the fall to plant tulips where they can be left undisturbed for ten or more years. This might mean dedicating a spot in the back of the border, or nestling them in amongst trees and shrubs, especially low junipers. Tulips will multiply and develop more flowers each spring if left undisturbed and fertilized each spring. It is only in a "make work garden" where you would want to lift tulips to replace them with annuals. In a true "no sweat" garden, you would treat tulips as perennials and leave them in a designated spot in the perennial border for years and years. If money and time are no object, you could treat tulips as annuals and toss them out when they are finished blooming.

If you accidentally put tulips in your one and only annual flower bed, dig them gently after blooming and move them with soil intact to the vegetable garden where they may be left until they have fully died back. Mark their location, and move them to a new permanent spot in late August or early September.

What height do you recommend cutting a lawn?

Leave it long. Root length is related to shoot length. The longer you can leave it, the more drought resistant it will be. This is especially true in mid-summer, when the longer grass shades and cools the roots more. Use the highest setting on your mower unless your lawn is a high traffic area. Like an old shag rug, long grass will be trampled and worn looking if it is continually walked on.

What type of potatoes are recommended on the prairies?

White, red, blue or banana! Essentially you have to decide what you would like to eat, and then you decide what to plant. There are all kinds of little known potatoes like the blue (a very small potato with a bluish tone due to purple colouring just under the skin) and the banana (which has a yellow, starchy texture and is best if baked). Among the common white potatoes, 'Viking' has been praised because it is white skinned (which in the potato world is actually brown), and the potatoes are good either boiled or baked. The red skinned potatoes like 'Norland', are ready earlier in the season, slightly more susceptible to potato scab, and best if boiled rather than baked.

Regardless of the type you grow, make sure you buy virus free stock fresh each spring so that you can avoid spreading disease from year to year. You wouldn't want a repeat of the great potato famine in your own back yard or pantry![13] Also, plant potatoes

"The two best defences for preventing weeds in lawns are mowing height and fertilization. In dry years, irrigation can be equally important.... Mowing heights should be maintained at two inches..."[14]

13. Reports from the Brooks Diagnostic Lab in the summer of 1993 reported Irish Potato Famine diseases in potatoes sent in for analysis. They highly encourage homeowners to grow certified disease free potatoes.

14. Cornell University Turfgrass Times, Spring 1994 Issue. Norman W. Hummel, Jr., "Organic Lawn Care: The Facts and Fallacies".

whole if you want to get a head start on the season. Cut potatoes might rot in the cool spring soil.

My soil always seems to turn clay-like even though I add peat moss and steer manure. I have also replaced my loam several times. What should I do?

Your efforts in the direction of improving organic matter have been good. You don't say how much you are adding, though, or if your soil cultivation practises are eroding your good efforts. Air acting on exposed organic matter encourages it to break down. Soil that is turned often is more exposed to air and you can expect organic matter to be decreased where soil is cultivated. Also, soil structure means much more than just the amount of organic matter. If soil is worked while it is wet, you quickly damage the fragile, almost crystal-like nature of soil particles. Once the structure is damaged, the soil quickly becomes dust-like or hard packed regardless of organic matter content.

No Sweat Gardening: Save time and energy by not digging your garden this spring:

"Tillage disrupts soil structure, brings up weed seeds, and produces excessive aeration and heating which speeds up the decomposition of organic matter and leaching of nutrients. After twenty years of no-till cropping, test plots at the Ohio Agricultural Research and Development Centre have three to ten times as much organic matter and available nutrients as tilled plots."[15]

Rather than replacing soil as it becomes "worn", try constantly topping up the soil surface with organics as you have been doing, except don't work the organics in beyond the top two centimetres of soil; let the soil critters do that for you. The result will be a deeper richer soil. Also, if the soil is most problematic in a vegetable garden, remember to rotate where you grow your peas and beans. If the top growth is removed but the roots left intact in the fall, these crops will add a great amount of decomposing organic matter to a deep soil depth. They quickly improve any soil they are grown in provided, once again, the soil is not turned too frequently and the benefits lost through rapid decomposition. Compost top-dressed in the garden always improves soil.

What annual flowers can I grow in a very shady back yard?

The biggest problems in deep shade are cool damp soils, and

15. Page 46, The Avant Gardener, Vol 25, No6, April 1993.

low light. If large trees are causing the deep shade, they could be thinned slightly. If the shade is caused by overhanging or shade casting buildings, I would suggest building raised planters which will alleviate the heavy wet soil syndrome. In these raised beds, try *Impatiens* which come in many shades including the brightest whites and pastels. Begonias, fuschias, and pansies also grow as annuals in shady spots.

Combine these best shade tolerant annuals with perennials such as *Lamium*, *Ajuga*, ferns, lily-of-the-valley, *Hostas*, corydalis, and bleeding hearts. Mix extra grit into the soil to encourage good drainage, and use cream edged varieties for a brighter look. Some of my favourite shade tolerant cream-edged plants include: variegated hostas (*Hosta* cultivar), variegated Veronica (*Veronica gentianoides* 'Variegata'), variegated false Solomon's seal (*Smilacina stellata* cultivar) and alpine lady's mantle (*Alchemilla alpina*).

How do you kill a Mayday once it has been cut down?

By constantly cutting the sprouting suckers as they appear. This is why it is important to cut a tree down when it is at its lowest energy levels so that it is weaker and easier to kill; this means cut it down just after it leafs out. See next questions for details.

Four mature poplar trees were cut down on my property before they leafed out. Now I am worried I will get all kinds of suckers; what should I do?

Ahhh, too bad you cut them down before they leafed out (see next question). Because the roots will now have a huge amount of stored energy in the form of sugar loaded sap, the tree will be searching for a way to use it. It will be sending out adventitious buds all across the root zone and from the stumps left in place. This will be a tremendous amount of work for you to remove the suckers as they appear for at least the duration of the summer.

You won't be able to successfully use systemic herbicides, because the roots of these poplars may have formed natural grafts between the roots of near-by poplars and any attempt to kill the suckers emerging with a systemic chemical will potentially do damage to other trees on yours and your neighbour's properties. Good Luck.

I have heard there is a mixture of diesel fuel and Killex useful in killing poplars. What is the correct ratio?

It is far better to kill a poplar when it is at its weakest point biologically than to hope a chemical will do the job fully on this sturdy, prairie hardy tree. The weakest point in a tree's life is just after it leafs out. It takes an enormous amount of energy to turn the engines on in a huge tree each spring, and this energy is taken at the expense of the rest of the tree. When the tree has just finished unfurling its leaves, most of the tree's energy will be used up so it is a good time to cut it down.

Follow-up by spraying with a 2,4-D Ester if you want to really be sure, or resort to the eco-friendly approach of clipping by hand any sprouts which spring from the trunk or near-by throughout the rest of the summer. If you are determined to remove this tree, keep after the suckers as they appear and have the stump of the main tree ground down as soon as you can. This replaces the old practise of killing trees when the time was convenient for people rather than biologically easiest. The older practise of combining Killex with diesel fuel was smelly and not always successful in killing the tree. Make sure to check label directions before using any chemical product.

In the past, I have had spider mites on my roses, and as well, the soil around my roses has become compacted and hard. How can I improve the roses and their soil without having to dig everything up to change the soil?

Overhead watering on sunny mornings is almost the single best cure for controlling spider mites on well grown roses. Many people are afraid of overhead watering because of leaf spot diseases, but if done in the morning just before a bright and sunny day, the danger of spreading leaf spot is greatly reduced. The overhead water should be just that... overhead. Pounding water shouldn't cut through the stems and leaves of roses but, rather, it should fall gently from above. Arrange this by placing your sprinkler on a stand above the roses. Spider mites can't tolerate humidity, so they will quickly move along or die. At the very least, they will be washed off the leaves and will have to crawl their way back up which will leave them drastically weakened.

To improve the soil, which needs to be very high in organic matter to support roses, try topdressing the soil with compost or manure at least once a year. One rose growing expert suggests spreading about nine pounds (4.5 kilograms) of composted manure around each rose bush in early June.[16] The compost is not worked into the soil because this could damage the roots. Instead, it is laid on top of the soil around the base of the bush. This "mulch" of manure will also help reduce spider mite populations, because it will make the roses healthier. Top-dressing may also be repeated in the fall.

When is the earliest time to place annuals in the garden?

Pansies, if hardened properly by growing at a low temperature of 15 degrees Celsius, may be put in the garden as early as the soil is workable in mid-April. Snapdragons may also be planted in cooler soils by early May if they are hardened. Other annuals are best left to late May or early June. Not being able to plant them does not mean not being able to buy them if you are sure you are able to look after them. They will need to be left in their flats outside during the day initially to get used to the elements including sun and wind. This is the process called "hardening off". Gradually finish hardening them to evening

Pansies can be put out in mid-April, if hardened properly.

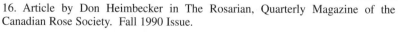

16. Article by Don Heimbecker in The Rosarian, Quarterly Magazine of the Canadian Rose Society. Fall 1990 Issue.

temperatures by leaving them out overnight. Eventually, reduce the moisture slightly as well, because this is part of the hardening process.

How many annuals will I need to buy for my garden? I have several beds of various sizes and just need to know how to figure out the right number.

It is probably best to work out the size of the flower bed first, then, based on that and the number needed per 100 square feet (approximately the same as ten square metres), you can calculate how many you need. Depending on how large the plants will ultimately get, you may wish to plant them anywhere from 15-20 centimetres apart in a triangular pattern. For instance, the tagetes marigolds sprawl and are usually planted 20 centimetres apart whereas the 'Boy O Boy' group are tiny and are spaced 15 centimetres apart. In ten square metres, this means a difference of 260 tagetes plants (with the wide spacing) and 460 'Boy O Boy' (if the tighter spacing is used). Unless you are landscaping very large beds, you shouldn't have to use this number of annuals anywhere but it's a good reference to use.

To decide how far apart to space plants use this approximate schedule:

Distance Between Plants:	Multiply square footage by:
10 cm (4")	6.0
15 cm (6")	4.0
20 cm (8")	2.2
22.5 cm (9")	1.8
30 cm (12")	1.0
45 cm (18")	.44
60 cm (24")	.25

The spacing of annuals depends on the kinds used. Here are some examples:

• *Ageratum*, *Alyssum*, lobelia, and other tiny border plants need to be spaced ten centimetres apart.

- Small marigolds ('Dainty Marietta', 'Boy o Boy'), pansies, stocks, dwarf zinnias, dianthus, and *Impatiens* are spaced 15 centimetres apart.

- Larger plants like the African marigolds (i.e., 'Perfection' series), petunias, asters, geraniums, snapdragons, flowering tobacco *(Nicotiana)*, cosmos, and sweet pea are spaced 20 centimetres apart.

Really large annuals like flowering kale and cabbage, lavatera, geraniums and sunflowers are spaced 25- 30 centimetres apart. Larger spacing is more common for larger perennials and one-gallon sized annuals.

There is an obvious cost savings if gardens with large annual flower beds use those types of flowers with a wider spacing.

Where can I get my soil tested?

There are many private soil testing labs listed in the phone book as well as the provincial soil testing labs which may be used by contacting the district agriculturist in your area. The costs vary somewhat so phone around.

I have heard a lot about the Austree from Australia. It is supposed to grow to an amazing size in a single year. Is it hardy?

Only the roots are hardy. This means top growth on this fast growing willow will not overwinter or even survive into late fall. It is not recommended in the home landscape because of this lack of top hardiness. You will be forever pruning dead, dry, brittle branches. You just knew there had to be a drawback to this "instant" tree didn't you?

Dew worms are making my lawn bumpy and lumpy. I really want to get rid of them.

You will be as lucky as the Australians were in ridding them-selves of an introduced pest, the rabbit. Any introduced pest comes **without** natural checks and balances, and it manages to thrive once it finds a niche. Older lawns are the perfect niche for dew worms, also known as night crawlers (*Lumbricus terestris*). These are shallow feeders which leave their castings on the soil surface but may burrow as deeply as two-and-a-half to three metres in winter or when conditions are unfavourable. Start heavy watering in the spring after aerating to make life uncomfortable for dew worms and to encourage them to move deeper or to a neighbour's drier lawn.

Chemicals have only a short term effect of making the lawn an uncomfortable spot. There is new hope with biological controls. We have to wait and see if the introduction of nematodes (see fungus gnat question in January) will be effective as a biological control for ground dwelling dew worms and slugs. Right now, the mite *Hypoaspis* may be somewhat successful, although it isn't specific to worms and may damage beneficial insects as well. This mite is available from retailers or horticultural wholesalers who offer biological controls.

Keeping your lawn long and well watered will also discourage worms in the short run this summer. Raking a centimetre or so of topsoil over the soil surface in the spring, after initial raking to remove thatch and aerating to open the soil, will help relieve some of the bumpiness and will make your lawn less dangerous for walking. A product such as "Clay Buster" works by breaking down the lumps and bumps caused by worm castings, so give that a try as well. Don't be thinking you can catch up these night crawlers and start your own worm composter. They aren't suitable because of their nature of alternating between very deep and shallow conditions.

Are the really short tulips I've seen in people's gardens hardy everywhere, and where can they be obtained?

The short tulips you've seen are probably "wild" tulips from Turkey and Syria. These have not been "improved" so have remained as small as their predecessors and you are right to enjoy them. They are darling. The smaller stature and flower size make them appealing for a smaller home garden and also often mean they will bloom earlier. Some are just like their wild ancestors, including: *Tulipa whittalii*, T. *urmuriensis*, T. *turkestanica*, and T. *suavolens*. Others, like the tulips classed as "waterlily tulips", are in the *Tulipa kaufmaniana* group and have been developed a bit more than other species tulips. Some of the varieties include 'Shakespeare', which is dark scarlet and yellow, and 'Ancilla', which is pink striped with pale yellow. They often have burgundy striped leaves which add extra interest.

The only downside to these dwarf tulips is they may emerge very early if planted in a warm site and then bloom when snow is still threatening. This will cut the length of bloom time considerably, but will not kill the tulips. They will often continue to bloom after the snow melts. Another problem is the dryness of soil some springs. While it is usually not advised to water most early emerging tulips, the early species types will show signs of drought on their flowers if they are not watered in the formative spring stages. Ideally then, they should be used where there is some shade or shelter from direct south sun.

The short tulip varieties can add interest to your garden.

What are the names of all the pink flowering shrubs in bloom in May?

The most dramatic of all the pink spring blooming shrubs is the double flowering plum (*Prunus triloba* 'Multiplex'). Others with pink blossoms before the leaves include the Nanking cherry (*Prunus tomentosa*) and Russian almond (*Prunus tenella*). All are leaf-hardy shrubs although the flower buds on the double flowering plum are not necessarily hardy, and in severe winters will be killed to below the snow line. This leaves a strange looking sight in the spring when all the pink blossoms are below a straight line which is perhaps a few inches or a few feet

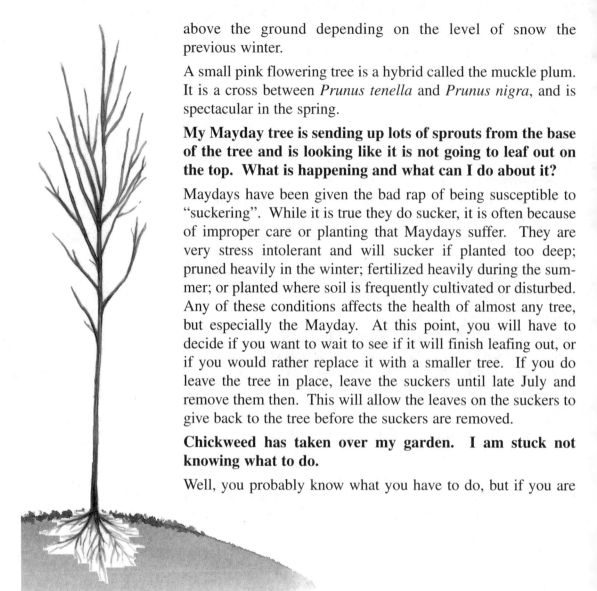

above the ground depending on the level of snow the previous winter.

A small pink flowering tree is a hybrid called the muckle plum. It is a cross between *Prunus tenella* and *Prunus nigra*, and is spectacular in the spring.

My Mayday tree is sending up lots of sprouts from the base of the tree and is looking like it is not going to leaf out on the top. What is happening and what can I do about it?

Maydays have been given the bad rap of being susceptible to "suckering". While it is true they do sucker, it is often because of improper care or planting that Maydays suffer. They are very stress intolerant and will sucker if planted too deep; pruned heavily in the winter; fertilized heavily during the summer; or planted where soil is frequently cultivated or disturbed. Any of these conditions affects the health of almost any tree, but especially the Mayday. At this point, you will have to decide if you want to wait to see if it will finish leafing out, or if you would rather replace it with a smaller tree. If you do leave the tree in place, leave the suckers until late July and remove them then. This will allow the leaves on the suckers to give back to the tree before the suckers are removed.

Chickweed has taken over my garden. I am stuck not knowing what to do.

Well, you probably know what you have to do, but if you are

Take care not to plant trees too deep, especially Maydays.

like most of us, you likely don't want to do it. Chickweed must be hand pulled and every little piece removed from the garden. Some people place clear plastic over the garden early in the spring to encourage all the chickweed seed on the surface to germinate so that when they do spend the time to weed, they know they are getting it all at once. Don't turn the soil after you have done this thorough weeding job, or you will bring more seed to the surface and recreate the problem. I know of people who refuse to turn their soil in the spring now because they have found keeping the soil untilled reduces the weeding.

What can I do about mysterious holes in my iris?

Not much unless you can see the culprit. If it is slug damage, try all the slug alternatives (see June). If you are lucky, the damage may have been caused by an insect just passing through the garden or plant, and it may not reoccur. There is absolutely no use spraying something you can't see, and a hole without the offending pest is like the scene of the crime, and it only twigs more questions without necessarily prompting solutions.

Are forsythia hardy in zone three and cooler? I would like to try one.

The leaf buds are reliably hardy, and the shrub will surely thrive if you grow one of the hardy cultivars such as 'Ottawa' forsythia or 'Northern Gold' forsythia. The flower buds are another story. They are formed on the plant the previous August and have to go through our long cold winters before they open. This puts them at risk because they are not as hardy as the leaf buds. It's a gamble whether you want to take up a spot in your garden for a plant that may or may not flower in the spring. Fortunately, they do flower approximately three out of five springs, and even in the cold non-flowering springs they usually offer a little colour from buds that are low enough to have been below the snow line in the winter. I would recommend it where you need a brilliant splash of yellow in April and where you have the space to plant other yellow alternatives such as crocus, auricula primulas or daffodils in case the forsythia doesn't make it.

What can be done for birch leafminer? I had it on my birch trees last year and want to prevent it from reappearing this spring.

Trees under stress attract insects, and most European introduced birch are out of place and therefore under stress here. If you have had birch leafminer before, you are right to assume you will get it again unless you have drastically changed the plant's growing conditions by mulching with a ten to 15 centimetre layer of bark or wood chip to the drip line of the tree. Keep soaker hoses on the plant for extended periods during the growing season. Otherwise, you will need a systemic insecticide.

The Northern Forest Research Centre in Edmonton reports the best controls for leafminer were obtained by applying undiluted dimethoate at the base of the infested tree in late May as directed on the label. One soil treatment was usually sufficient to control all three species of leafminer in one season. At least one of the insects causing leafminer symptoms overwinters in the fallen leaves in the winter, so raking up the leaves in the fall will also help control the problem to some extent. (See also March).

Birch leafminer is a common problem. Improving a tree's growing conditions can help prevent insect attacks.

Are red edges on spruce a sign of spider mite?

Not necessarily. This could be a sign of winter damage due to drying or it could be a fungal disease. Use a hand lens or any magnifying glass you have available to check the inner leaves of the spruce for the obvious mites on the leaf undersides. You may also notice the obvious webbing when the sun shines on the moistened branches. If you have a fungal disease, such as needle cast (several types, all in the *Ascomycetes* class), the second year infected needles will be a reddish-straw colour with black/grey spots along the needle midribs. Needle rust (at least six different species) appear as rusty, knobby blobs along discoloured needles.

If you see this little fellow, your problems are related to spider mites, which are common on many plants including spruce trees.

I have a question about bringing my dahlias out of storage. They still look firm and good.

Pot them up immediately. They can't be planted outside right away, because dahlias can't tolerate frost, but they will do much better if allowed to begin growing indoors and then moved outside in early June. If the storage tubers (the part you put away for the winter) are shrivelled at all they may not regrow. Only place an inch (two centimetres) or so of soil over the tuber when it is potted and then water lightly. Don't keep the soil soggy but add enough water to stimulate regrowth.

How do you prepare for laying sod?

Ideally, the same way you prepare for seeding a lawn. This means adequate soil improvement to a depth of 20-30 centimetres followed by raking to remove rocks and larger debris, and finally, rolling with a rented roller to even out and pack down the soil. The soil preparation is the key. At least 98% of the effort in sodding should be in the soil preparation. It will be easy to maintain a lawn in the future if the soil is prepared properly now.

The first time to apply chemicals to control birch leafminer in the spring is when the garland spirea (Spiraea x arguta) blooms. Add this spirea to your garden if you have a birch tree so you will never have to guess at your timing again. If you don't have a garland spirea, make sure to wait until your birch tree leaves are fully open before you spray.

The first step in preparing for a lawn in a new home is to water the soil heavily. If the home was built in the winter, there may be 60 centimetres or more sinking where the water and power lines have gone into the house. It's a huge disappointment to have the lawn sink **after** the sod has been laid, so do this heavy watering before the rough grading is finished. Water, water, water.

If topsoil is easily accessible and inexpensive, the second step in preparing for sod is to order as deep a layer of topsoil as you can afford. Fantastic lawns and shrub beds often have 30 centimetres or more topsoil beneath them. The ideal loam will hold its shape when squeezed together in your hand if it is slightly moist, and then crumble apart when it is touched. A soil with too much clay will hold its shape and not crumble apart, and a soil with too much sand will not hold together at all when squeezed.

If the topsoil you receive appears low in organic matter, add peat moss and mix it in with a rototiller. A small amount of high phosphorus fertilizer (the second number listed on the fertilizer bag) may be tilled in with the peat moss. Rough raking will slope the soil away from the house. Once the ground has settled and the rough grade has been finalised, finer raking may begin. This will remove pebbles and roots of weeds just before the final stage of rolling. After rolling, re-rake spots that seem low, so the surface is even throughout and gradually sloping away from the buildings. Lay sod to stagger the seams. Water. Don't walk on new sod for at least a week to allow the sods to knit and soil to firm up. Do not spray with any chemicals for at least the first year.

What is the best support system for taller growing perennials like delphiniums?

There are several ways to support perennials but I prefer the metal rings that can be pulled up out of the ground as the plant grows to provide the support where and when it is needed. You can either fabricate these yourself from #9 wire purchased at a hardware store, or buy the premade systems like the "links" system offered at garden centres.

Last year my delphiniums had a worm in the flower heads that ate the flowers. I can't find this bug listed in any of the gardening books or references. What is it and how do I get rid of it?

What are these web worms on delphiniums and how can we control them so the flowers aren't all chewed up?

In both cases, the problem is the delphinium leaf tier (pronounced 'tire'). You won't see it mentioned much because it is a native prairie insect which normally feeds on our native delphiniums and is probably shocked at the size of the feast available in our home garden cultivated delphiniums.

In late May to early June this little insect becomes noticeable. Because it is a "local" problem caused by a "local" insect it isn't usually listed in the national or international gardening books. According to Olds College entomologist, Ernest Mengerson, these insects are the larval stage of a native moth *Polychrysia moneta*.[17] In the wild, the caterpillar feeds on our native larkspurs, and in our gardens it goes for ornamental delphiniums which are very closely related to our natives. Ernest believes it is the native insect causing the problem because he has found parasites on this insect where he has found native larkspur. And in the rainy summer of 1993 not a single larvae matured to a pupal or adult stage in my garden although I was hoping one would so that I could photograph it! This probably means poor weather encourages the parasites and discourages the maturation of the moth.

There is probably only a single generation of this insect each year, which should make it very easy to control with cultural rather than spray strategies. The larvae begin hatching and eating shortly after the leaves appear in the spring (probably because the eggs are laid in the soil at the base of the plant).

17. Personal discussions with Ernest Mengerson via Anita Schill of Olds College, Olds, Alberta.

The eating becomes noticeable by mid-May when the leaves are obviously "tied" together, droppings accumulate, and the growing larvae (caterpillars) become more obvious.

The best control is to mow the foliage back to within four to six centimetres above the ground when the plant has reached a height of 30 centimetres tall. Make sure to send the young trimmed leaves to the trash and not to the compost where the caterpillars may crawl away. If you have missed cutting the plant back when it was small the summer alternative is to hand pick affected leaves and dispose of the larvae. This insect is not a problem everywhere every year on every plant, so there is really no need to use preventative sprays, especially since the cultural control is so simple.

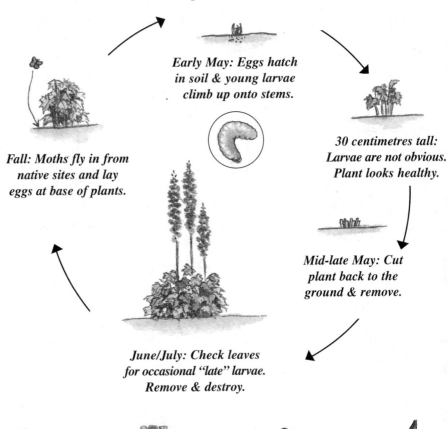

Early May: Eggs hatch in soil & young larvae climb up onto stems.

Fall: Moths fly in from native sites and lay eggs at base of plants.

30 centimetres tall: Larvae are not obvious. Plant looks healthy.

Mid-late May: Cut plant back to the ground & remove.

June/July: Check leaves for occasional "late" larvae. Remove & destroy.

There are white, mealy bug looking things on my spruce. What are they?

This is one of the many pests attracted to spruce in the spring. It is part of the life cycle of the adelgid gall forming aphid (genera including *Adelges* and *Pineus*). Some people think the crawling stage looks like bits of cotton fluff; this white "stuff" is really just a waxy protective coat over the sap sucking little adelgids which swap life between different evergreens depending on the species in question. The second, totally different looking phase of this insect's life are the galls which form at the tips of branches. One common and well known adelgid is the cooley spruce gall adelgid, *Adelges cooleyi*. It seems to alternate life between spruce and Douglas fir but this is now under debate. Several other kinds are also known, and the effect is more or less the same. One stage is white and fluffy while the other is gall forming.

The white fluffy stage may be sprayed with high pressure water, soapy water, or a light oil solution of soap and water. The gall forming stage should be cut off as soon as galls begin forming, otherwise the insects will mature by late summer and go on to infect other trees or reinfect the same tree. Unfortunately, the galls are often unnoticed until they are emptied of their insect companions, and removing them after they are emptied in the late fall or winter will not help reduce the pest in your yard. Systemic insecticides are largely useless and unregistered for use on evergreens, and are especially useless against this insect pest.

What evergreens are hardy in northern gardens?

There are several "kinds" (genera) of hardy evergreens. Evergreen shrubs include the following genera: junipers, cedars, dwarf spruce, yews, dwarf fir, microbiota, and pine. Evergreen trees include spruce, fir, pine, and Douglas fir. In each group, there are many species and many more cultivars.

The species are quite variable as you would expect of plants of the same kind but with different genetic variability; this differs from plants of the same cultivar. They are identical, they have been cloned. Think of the wide variation among mugo pines (*Pinus mugo*). Some are tight and short needled while others are rambling and loose. Some of this variation is a result of cultural differences or the care the shrubs are given. Much, though, is just an expression of the natural differences among plants of the same species.

Compare the differences in the mugo pines to the identical nature of plants which are the same **cultivar** like blue chip juniper *(Juniperus horizontalis* 'Blue Chip'). All blue chips are cloned from a 'mother' plant. They will all be dwarf, compact but upfacing, blue junipers which turn purple in the winter. If you want a specific look in your yard and that look is blue chip, then order blue chip. It will be the same in your yard as it is in a botanical garden or garden centre.

There is no one list of evergreens guaranteed to grow in every northern situation, but cultivars in the *Juniperus horizontalis, Juniperus scopulorum*, *Pinus mugo*, or *Picea pungens* groups are the toughest and most likely to succeed. These basic plant names will be on the tags and will be followed by cultivar names such as 'Yukon Belle' as in *Juniperus horizontalis* 'Yukon Belle'. I hope there will be further development among plant breeders to select trees and shrubs from northern forests and mountains to increase the number of native, hardy evergreen shrubs on the market.

Is it true that poplars will damage basements and harm the lawn?

It is true that poplar roots as well as willow roots will grow where there is underground moisture. If there is a break or leak in a water line, the roots may grow towards and even into the pipe. I have never heard of roots creating the break in a pipe or a basement but they often take advantage of an opportunity when it presents itself.

Poplars may appear to damage a lawn where the two are in direct competition. A poplar planted too deep, for instance, will tend to produce main support roots which grow slightly upwards. These appear above the soil or even break through asphalt. It is usually best to start by planting the tree correctly, and then keep competing lawns away from the drip line of the tree. This will be best for both the lawn and the tree.

What grows in Calgary?

Thousands of different taxa, i.e., different plants, grow in Calgary. We have one of the harshest climates because of the very dry and often cold winters followed by unexpected warm spells which dry both soil and plant. At least a couple hundred different cultivars of annual flowers; several thousand different cultivars of perennials; hundreds of tree and shrub cultivars; and many other groundcovers, vines, and succulents will grow. We are considered a zone three but that is more limiting for trees and shrubs than perennials. The Hamilton Botanical Garden, for instance, has over 1500 different lilacs on their property. There is no reason to believe that all these lilacs wouldn't grow here. Everyone should visit their closest public garden or park to begin assembling a starter list of plants hardy in their area.

The new leaves on my green ash tree have been frozen. Will the tree die?

Probably not. Green ash, *Fraxinus pennsylvanica*, are quite hardy. Even though the first buds were lost to frost there are many more dormant buds which will now push through. It is not ideal for a plant to be put under this type of stress too often but there is nothing that can be done about freak cold weather this late in May. If any tree or shrub in your yard regularly leafs out and then gets frozen, you may have to take a harder look at this. Try a different tree, try mulching to keep the soil cool, or try shading the tree somehow. Repeated spring frost damage will ruin the shape of trees.

How do you plant a waterlily to place in an outdoor pond with a concrete base?

Because ponds with fibreglass, concrete or even rubber liners cannot be planted into directly, many people plant waterlilies in a pot first and then place the whole pot in the pond. Once the waterlily is potted up, cover the soil surface with landscape fabric and then four centimetres of gravel to prevent the soil from floating away. Submerge the whole pot into the water so the leaves are suspended in the water rather than hanging over the edge of the pot. To get the plant and pot to the right height in the pond, many people place old bricks beneath the pot. See diagram in March.

What do you do about berries hanging on a mountain ash tree in the spring?

Nothing. If the waxwings and other birds missed eating your berries this past winter, they may still come by for them. If they are really bothering you, you could cut them off, but this is a lot of work and it won't hurt the tree to leave them on.

There are white spots on my caragana leaves. What is this?

It could be spider mites which you can confirm by looking at the underside of the leaves with a magnifying glass. The mites are tiny and red, and will be moving around. Alternately, it could be a leaf sucking "plant bug". Again, check the leaves for signs of insect damage. Most insects and mites are easily controlled with a soapy solution; read the directions on the Safers Insecticidal Soap label. Luckily mites rarely kill caragana, so you may decide not to bother with a spray of any kind but start misting your trees occasionally when it gets hot. If you don't have mites, you could have powdery mildew which

---

18. From Hortideas May 1992, 9(5), pg 51.

is a fungus disease. This looks like a light dusting of flour on the upper leaf surface, and is controlled by changing the pH of the leaf surface. Recipes for controlling this fungus, if that's what you have, are on pages 138-139.

Company "X" pruned my trees last winter and ruined them. What can I do now?

Nothing really. It's buyer beware with tree care companies because there are so many factors involved in tree care; it's not a simple product like a garden fork or a novel. It is hard to know how the job will come out until it is done. This is why I strongly encourage people to check references of people doing pruning and even ask for addresses where pruning has been done so you can go and have a look for yourself to make sure the finished work is what you expect. Next, make sure the company has a certified arborist on staff, and preferably talk to that person yourself before the job begins, to ensure the arborist will be on site during the work. A wronged tree is like Humpty Dumpty; it is impossible to put it back together again. Prevention is the only hope. In defence of the tree care trade, I have heard of tree owners who insist on a tree being topped or otherwise mistreated.

Rather than passing up the work, the tree companies may comply with the owner's wishes and commit a crime against trees. A good arborist should be able to explain to the tree owner why topping is not a recommended practice. They should avoid doing something incorrect like tree topping because their company name will then be implicated in such a practice. A reputable arborist might hand the saw and ladder to the owner and say "You'll have to do it yourself; I don't want my name ruined".

To make sure you have tree work done correctly, learn a bit about pruning yourself (see diagrams in February) and ask for qualifications and references when hiring out pruning.

What are the hardiest types of ferns?

The ostrich ferns (*Matteuccia struthiopteris* and *Matteuccia pensylvanica*) are the most commonly found ferns in prairie gardens. The first is introduced from Europe and the second is native to northern forests. Both adapt well on the north side of the house where they reach a height of 45-60 centimetres. They tend to brighten up a dark corner because their leaves are a light lime green.

Other ferns worth trying include a few of our natives such as parsley fern (*Cryptogramma acrostichoides*), lady fern (*Athyrium filix-femina*), fragile fern (*Cystopteris fragilis*), rocky mountain woodsia (*Woodsia scopulina*) and spreading wood fern (*Drypoteris* species).[19] They are best obtained from specialty growers or fern spore exchanges.

Is it okay to add manure to the vegetable garden?

Not necessarily. If there are traces of herbicides in the hay the cattle were fed, this will instantly become obvious in tomato and potato plants which are indicator plants for herbicides. Even without trace chemicals, manure causes a few other problems in vegetable gardens. Potatoes tend to get scab where manure was used, and carrots get extremely hairy. This is all true only in cases where **too much** manure was used. Limit quantities to a few centimetres topdressed over the soil in the fall. It will leach gradually by spring and will not be right in the root zone immediately, so will not adversely affect the root crops. In all cases, make sure to use well rotted manure and brace yourself for weeds. Many weed seeds manage to escape damage in the rotting/composting process and germinate quickly once in the garden.

Even though this sounds like manure is a negative, it isn't. It improves soil like nothing else and can be purchased

19. Mosses and Lichens of Northwest North America, D. Vitt, J. Marsh, and R. Bovey. Lonepine Press 1988.

pasteurised at garden centres which means the weed seeds will be dead. Within a few years of topdressing garden soil with either compost or manure, the texture and workability of the soil changes almost miraculously as it becomes soft, friable, crumbly, and easy draining.

What is the best apple tree to plant for the home garden? We want something good to eat fresh because we don't want to bother with a lot of freezing and canning.

My long time favourite is the Norland apple which is sweet and crisp and fairly long keeping. Newer types of apples now on the market include:

- Norcue - medium sized, early season, yellow apple with red stripes. Keeps up to ten weeks.

- Noret - small, red apple which is very tasty, and stores for up to six weeks.

- Norlove - small, early season, red and yellow apple which is good for eating, cooking and juicing. Will keep four weeks.

- Other notable early apples include: Parkland, Sunnybrook, and Westland.

If you want to risk growing later season apples, the Sprout catalogue[20] lists many more worth trying. Applecrabs and crabapples are slightly smaller but also excellent in the home garden, and are also worth trying.

My mountain ash tree is dying. The new leaves are very small and the twigs are curled under slightly. It looks bad. What is happening, and why?

Dr. Shigo tells me it has been common knowledge since the late 1800's that high use of nitrogen is linked to death by fireblight among susceptible trees. Mountain ash is one of those trees and

---

20. The Sprout Farm Catalogue is a highly recommended mail order and farm source of hardy fruit trees. Their farm is north of Edmonton, Alberta, and the owners are highly knowledgeable on all aspects of fruit tree production.

the symptoms you describe are classic. Early in the spring, around the time apples are in bloom, honey bees spread this bacterial disease from blossom to blossom. It then spreads rapidly down the small flowering spurs and into the branches. Flies and ants continue to spread the disease by picking up the sweet bacterial ooze on their feet and then travelling off to new, uninfected sites and trees.

The newest, lushest branch growth is most affected and soon the typical "shepherds crooking" you described, as well as sunken, brown patches on the main bark, will appear. In high humidity conditions, you may also see yellow ooze-like drops of honey on the bark. The active bacteria will be 30 centimetres below the visible damage, so if the main trunk is damaged, the tree should be removed and burned or brought to the dump. If the wood is not removed from the property, it will continue to be an infection site for other plants in the rose family including cotoneaster shrubs, apple trees, cherries, plums, and apricots.

If the tree can safely be pruned, make sure to wash the shears between each cut with a 3% bleach solution to prevent spreading the disease. Also, spray mixtures to kill this bacterial disease are available at the garden centres, but they are only effective if used on the tree when it is in bloom. They will only prevent further infection, not improve currently diseased tissue. There are tree implants for fireblight on the market, but they are not recommended.

I would like more information on vines in this area. How do you grow them and which ones are worth trying?

There are hardy, woody vines which regrow from the woody, long lived branches; perennial vines which regrow from the ground every year; and annual vines which must be planted or seeded each spring. Although there are not too many kinds at this time, new types are always being tested in home and public gardens. Here is a selection of each kind:

Hardy woody vines:

• Virginia creeper and Engelman Virginia creeper (*Parthenocissus quinquefolia* and *Parthenocissus quinquefolia 'Engelmannii'*) - The best feature of these vines is their outstanding fall colour. The leaves turn brilliant crimson most years which is especially important if you don't have other sources of fall colour in your yard. These may be hard to establish initially, and I have heard the complaint occasionally they are "not hardy". What this means is they are hard to establish. Try them in a spot with at least half a day of sun and mulch the roots as soon as they are planted. If you don't have a cedar or brick house which the Engelman form can cling to, or if you are growing plain Virginia creeper, give these vines a support trellis or guide lines. Problems include powdery mildew on the leaves when over fertilized. Use the powdery mildew baking soda solution listed on page 138.

• Dropmore scarlet honeysuckle (*Lonicera x Brownii* 'Dropmore Scarlet') - A hummingbird highlight, this vine is absolutely loaded with tubular flowers once established. Unfortunately, it is often also loaded with aphids which are attracted to the nectar rich flowers which drip and leak their load of nectar. Bees, with their too-short tongues, chew through the base of the flowers before sipping the nectar from the floral tube. This woody vine may not be fully hardy on all sites and is very slow to cover an arbour or gazebo; it is recommended instead for a small section of trellis along an east facing wall. Honeysuckle does best when supported to the trellis with occasional tying.[21] Do not prune in the first several years except in June to remove winterkill.

• Bittersweet (*Celastris scandens*) - Grows more like a rambling informal shrub than a woody vine in our climate. After several years in the gardens of the Calgary Zoo, it has

Dropmore scarlet honeysuckle is a hardy woody vine in northern gardens.

21. Try using "Floraltie", a foam-coated wire which won't damage the bark. Pantyhose work well too.

never reached the top of the six-foot tall (two metre) trellis. It may be worth attempting on the hot spots of the prairies like southern Manitoba and Medicine Hat. The cold winters don't kill them in Calgary, but the growth is so slow in our cool summers they never amount to much.

• Clematis (*Clematis* cultivars) - The most fantastic blossoms come from this group of woody climbers; they have really earned a spot in our gardens. The only tricky thing about clematis is their need for cool feet and sunny tops. Gardeners achieve this by planting them on the north side of a fence and training the top growth through to the south. Alternately, any good bright garden spot will be a good place for clematis as long as a large rock or piece of paving stone is placed over the roots to keep them cool.

If you want to keep it simple with clematis, try the types that bloom on "new wood". This way, if they die back completely over winter, they will still resprout and bloom in the summer. Also, it means the vines may be cut back to the ground each spring. This makes it easier for beginners who may not be able to tell the difference between new and old wood when pruning. As you get more experience, try the varieties that bloom on new and old wood. These are only pruned lightly in the spring. Finally, if you have an excellent spot which is warm and protected near a building, try the Jackmanii types which bloom on old wood i.e., the branches, leaf buds, and flower buds have to overwinter or you won't get any blooms.

Luckily, most tags at the nursery carry the basic pruning information or tell you when the plant will bloom. From this cryptic code, you can figure out how to prune and whether to buy. A label might say, for instance, "blooms from summer to fall" which means it blooms on new wood. Or, if it says "blooms in spring and again in summer or fall", this means it blooms on new and old wood. Finally, if the tag says "blooms in early spring", you are forewarned that it may not bloom at all on the prairies and it should never be pruned in the winter or planted out on an arbour away from a building.

- Hardy kiwi (*Actinidia kolomikta* cvs.) - If growing a curiosity is your goal, then it might be worth growing this "still alive and hanging in there" vine, although I can't see tying up space in my own yard for a plant that does little else but offer a challenge. There is definitely a difference between living and thriving, and I would place this tenuous choice in the latter category.

- River-bank grape (*Vitis riparia*) - Try this where you can obtain a hardy plant from a local nursery. It has beautiful broad leaves and long, self-clinging tendrils. It appreciates full sun.

Perennial vines:

Climbing nightshade (*Solanum dulcamara*) - This vine simultaneously blooms and fruits in mid-summer to late summer which offers a startling contrast between the very intensely red, mini-tomato style fruit and the bright purple flowers. If it wasn't so toxic it would likely be more widely used. It is very easy from cuttings which start within days in water, and it is also easy from seed, which spreads on its own via the tiny fruits. It is so easy from seed, I kept finding seedlings four years after I removed the main plant and paved over the area where I had it confined.

River-bank grape is an underutilized hardy vine.

Climbing nightshade is a quick climbing vine which may reach heights of three to five metres in a single season, easily covering an arching arbour or side and top of a gazebo. All parts are **toxic**, and the truly delightful little fruits make it too tempting where children might play to realistically consider it in most home gardens.

- Hops (*Humulus lupulus*) - The monk's choice as beer flavouring is also Donna's choice as a great perennial vine. Before 1850, monks brewed beer with almost any flower they could find including tansy, sage, ginger, and ground ivy; hops was only one of many choices.[22] Trouble was, the finished beer always had a different taste, depending on the source of floral flavouring. Hops became the universal choice for brewing because they proved hardy wherever beer was made (i.e., everywhere); they are still the flower of choice today.

As a perennial vine, hops rapidly sprawls up a trellis or line to reach four to five metres in a summer and amply covers the tallest arch or screens the widest deck. Their delightful flower clusters, although only green, hang down gracefully from the vines, especially from vines that have sprawled overhead to cover the roof of an outdoor gazebo or deck.

Hops can't tolerate any working of the soil around the roots, so must be planted where they are undisturbed. The light green leaves make an excellent contrast in texture and colour to other less tropical looking plants, and the flowers provide a fine, unusual scent.

• Perennial sweet pea (*Lathyrus latifolius*) - If you love sweet peas but hate the annual effort, this vine is for you. Blooming in a range of shades from white to pink to dark purple, these hardy perennials are making a comeback in old fashioned gardens and almost anywhere a vine is needed. Be careful not to disturb the roots with shallow cultivating.

• Perennial morning glory (*Calystegia hederacea* 'Flore Pleno') - With bright pink flowers all summer long, this vigorous, perennial vine will surely cover any arbour or trellis in a hurry. In fact, it may be too vigorous, so keep an eye on it and don't let it get out of bounds. Super for covering chain-link fences or gazebos.

Annual vines:

• Canary bird vine (*Tropaeolum peregrinum*) - With flowers that look like bright little canaries, this light coloured, fast

---

22. Flower of the Vine, Raymond Sokolov, Natural History, 1/92. pages 81-83.

growing annual is suitable for almost any full sun garden entrance or fence. The seeds mature quickly even in cool summer evenings, and will scatter on their own and regrow the following season which makes this the most perennial-like annual of the bunch. Clip off seeds which form before the end of July to coerce longer and later blooming.

• Sweet pea (*Lathyrus odoratus*) - Perhaps the most ideal "kitchen garden" vine with its heavenly aroma and long blooming habit. Sweet peas combine intense flower colours with intense scent and they are easy to grow, too. Start early indoors or buy as a bedding plant where the season is extremely short. The minimal need? Try presoaking seed before placing out in the garden.

• Scarlet runner bean (*Phaseolus coccineus*) - Bright red flowers attractive to hummingbirds are the trademark of these quick growing annuals. They suffer from rotting before they germinate in cool soil, so are probably best presoaked or preferably started in advance indoors for best results.

I'd like to know if it's feasible to raise a cutleaf Japanese maple outdoors here? If so, what are its requirements? It is one of the loveliest plants we've ever seen.

It wouldn't be hardy outdoors in the winter but if you had it in a container on casters, you could grow it like European royalty grew oranges.[23] Ideally, use a fairly large wooden box to begin with and overwinter it in a cool greenhouse which is allowed to get down near zero in the winter but not much colder. The leaves will drop off in the fall, and it will only need occasional watering while dormant. When greenhouse temperatures are warmed up to grow bedding plants in mid-winter, the maple will leaf out again and be ready for bringing outdoors again in spring. It is available from mail order catalogues in warmer climates

23. In European cities which were too cold to raise oranges outdoors year round, citrus trees were grown in large wooden boxes and simply brought into conservatories in the fall.

"(as insurance against catastrophic losses)... no single (tree) species should make up more than 5% of the total number of trees in a city area."[24]

like those in lower mainland British Columbia and Ontario.

Larger greenhouses in almost all areas order plants from California wholesalers and will often include a special order from an individual on their order. Ask right away because May is a peak shipping season for greenhouses.

Is there anything special to know about pruning a cedar?

In northern gardens, the plants sold as cedars are usually arbivortae which are cultivars of *Thuja occidentalis*. They are evergreen so may be pruned whenever the wood is not frozen. To shape them in a certain fashion, prune when dormant and then again when the new growth has finished flushing in June.

Most cultivars already have a specific shape, so try to start with a plant that is likely to grow the way you want it to right from the beginning. 'Wareana' and 'Woodwardia' cultivars are ball-shaped but tend to be more upright than wide; 'Brandon' is narrow and columnar; 'Little Giant'[25] is an improved and extremely hardy small globe shape; and 'Techny' is a loose, upright, informal shape. There is hardly any need to prune these plants because of their natural tendencies towards a specific shape, and if the pruning is directed towards changing the shape dramatically, i.e., turning a loose upright form into a tight dwarf ball, you will probably fail. Instead, keep the pruning minimal, and trim back only the occasional branch that grows too far out of bounds.

Occasionally, junipers are mistakenly called cedars. This is especially true of the "cedar" used to line "cedar chests". The scented and wonderfully aromatic wood comes from a juniper, *Juniperus virginiana*, which is listed as a zone five and is rare

---

24. Recommendation of Dr. Nina Bassuk, Program Leader at the Urban Horticulture Institute, Cornell University.

25. Little Giant Cedar was proven hardy throughout Alberta after extensive testing by the Landscape Alberta Nursery Trades Association (Lanta) and Alberta Agriculture. It is highly recommended throughout the prairies. It is one of Lanta's Plant Promotion Plants for 1996.

in northern gardens. Hardy, upright junipers such as *Juniperus scopulorum* 'Blue Heaven' are sometimes sheared slightly to make their naturally upright form a little more compact. It is also possible to start with a naturally tighter form, such as *Juniperus scopulorum* 'Medora', if you want to reduce your pruning efforts.

What types of things can be put in my compost pile?

No meat or fats which may attract animals, but almost all green materials will work. Try all your kitchen greens such as apple cores, peelings, old lettuce, ends of cabbage, orange peels, grapefruit rinds, bean nibs, coffee grounds, entire pumpkins after Halloween, eggs, and crusts of bread. There isn't any green waste from your kitchen that won't work. Add to that all the garden waste such as flowers that have been removed when they fade, pinched ends of perennials, old perennials cut back, carrot tops, potato plant tops, leaves raked from trees, and clippings from the lawn. The big bulky stuff like corn husks, dry leaves, and spent sunflower stalks nicely balance the nitrogen rich green stuff like carrot tops and lawn clippings. There is a specific formula for success but hardly anyone has a formula-perfect amount of compost material ready to add in sequence.[26] If the pile is too stinky, you either aren't turning it enough or you have too much of the nitrogen rich green stuff and too little of the dry, carbon rich stuff. Because there is such a load of carbon available in the fall as dry leaves, many people bag the extras and save them to mix with the lawn grass which is available in quantity in the summer.

Ideally, the pile should be turned two to three times a week to add oxygen and keep the smell down because the microorganisms that smell most are those that thrive without oxygen. The turner/spinner composters that allow you to turn the works daily

26. "The ideal compost pile has a carbon to nitrogen ratio of about 25:1..." Page 9, Backyard Composting To Reduce Household Waste, Alberta Action On Waste leaflet. Call 1-800-463-6326 for a free copy.

produce the fastest results because they encourage the best mixing of materials and air. A pile never turned and always topped up will never be "done", but will gradually sink over the years and appear to be done in portions at least - the bottom portion that is hardest to reach.

Some people pre-compost by blending their kitchen scraps before adding them to the pile, or they run their lawn mower over their outdoor leaves and wastes to chop them up. This helps considerably in speeding up composting. The smaller particles burn up quicker and literally vanish within a few weeks. Renting a chipper/grinder in the fall is another way to speed up the decomposition of the large, coarse waste such as corn stalks and sunflower stems. Make sure to add any leftover lawn fertilizer (unless it has a herbicide component) or any aged or non-aged barnyard waste if it is available. I find the material waste from our guinea pigs is great in the compost. Warning: don't compost the droppings of any carnivores such as dogs and cats.

If you can't set up a formal compost system due to bears and other wildlife, try incorporating your ground and chopped compostables right into the garden by digging a small trench in the soil and burying everything. Alternatively, try a totally enclosed composter or even indoor vermiculture.

Where can I get a gentian plant? I haven't been able to find these anywhere.

Gentians are often sold in specialty perennial catalogues or shops that specialise in alpines even though they aren't all alpines. There are native gentians on the prairies. If you have trouble finding gentians locally, try the specialized mail order houses like Gardenimport, White Flower Farms, or Hortico.[27] If you join an alpine plant group, like the Scottish or North American Rock Garden Societies, you will be eligible to send

27. See appendix for address and phone numbers of suppliers and plant societies.

for free seeds each winter and gentians are usually included on the list. If you want to go through the effort of importing plants from the United States, you will need certificates of health (Phytosanitary certificates) from the supplier and may also have to pay for Agriculture Canada inspections once the plants arrive. This really adds to the time and cost, so it really is best to buy within Canada or start from seed if possible.

Fortunately, there has been a trend lately for the local garden centres to include more and more unique rock garden and alpine plants, so keep checking and asking at your local greenhouses.

I have a plant called mother-of-thyme. Is it edible? It smells just like thyme spice.

Yes, I use it fresh frequently and have even dried some for use in the fall and winter. The flavour is more intense before mother-of-thyme (*Thymus praecox*) flowers but it is not as intense as the very fine leaved *Thymus vulgaris*.

When do you prune *Alyssum saxatile*, the basket-of-gold plant?

It doesn't really need pruning but many people cut this perennial back after it blooms to keep it neat and tidy looking. It is also available in dwarf or compact forms which are less work. It is called basket-of-gold for its overwhelming show of yellow flowers in the spring. A newer and more correct Latin name is *Aurinia saxatalis*. ◢

Chapter Six

J · U · N · E

Settling In

*P*erennials are spilling over with bloom, and the occasional evening is warm. It's tempting to imagine we live in a warm climate complete with pleasant weather when we look around and admire our handiwork. Most of the "spring" planting is done, but the beauty of June is that it's not too late for a few last minute purchases, so indulge yourself. Anyone with a rock garden or early blooming perennials will be enjoying the continuing peak of blossom this month. In the wild, the prairie crocuses are just finished, the roses are beginning, and the blue flax overlaps between the two.

Trouble will be lurking on the introduced or less than stress-free evergreens in the back yard. It may be tempting to bring out the chemical big guns, but often enough a thorough misting with water and soap will dislodge the pestiest spruce problems. I try to reserve time for bird watching. If I see the orioles pecking at the branches of my spruce trees, I know I have sawflies and then I'm facing a dilemma. Should I take the food out of these beautiful birds' mouths by spraying or just leave it alone one more year?

Summer pruning begins to shape the early spring blooming shrubs we didn't want to clip in winter for fear of accidentally removing flower buds. Have a look at your spring flowering double flowering plums, forsythia, or lilacs to see if they need a little renewal or thinning now. Pruning these spring bloomers after they have fully leafed out will help ensure flowers next spring.

Take care of the little weeding problems before they explode, and promise yourself a daily moment in your hammock. You really need this time to survey your handiwork, and in a critical moment or two, evaluate the garden for balance and beauty. Plan to add a few more spots of colour where the earliest phlox and hepatica have left green spots. It's not too late to add a planter on the deck with a scented geranium or evening scented stock.

Rock gardens spill over with colourful creeping and sprawling plants. Hanging baskets are out on their perches, tomatoes are

Geranium, Pelargonium cultivars (left).

To Do This Month:
🌿 *Plant a late crop of lettuce.*
🌿 *Plant potatoes after the risk of frost is past.*
🌿 *Put your late and tender flowering plants in the garden.*
🌿 *Prune in June.*

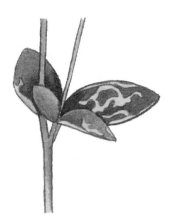

Leafminers burrowing within the leaves of columbines may be controlled by picking off and destroying affected leaves.

planted, and it's beginning to look a lot like summer. There may still be a hint of chill in the air where altitude or latitude keep our garden enthusiasm in check, but almost everywhere the days are bright and the blooms are brighter than we ever remember them. We are face to face with colours impossible to recreate in our mind like gentian blue with wallflower orange.

The blooms are peaking but so are the bugs, insects, and molluscs. We start to divide our time between enjoying and tending. The last potatoes are in the ground, and the early blossoms on the annuals give promise of bigger splashes of colour and taste to come. Leap into summer but don't work too hard. This is the beginning of the season of payback.

What do you need to do to wild rose seedlings to induce them to flower? My father took some seeds to England and they grew like weeds with lots of green but no flowers.

Tell him to stop fertilizing because a plant growing in a very fertile soil will have little need to blossom. In England, a rich soil combined with plenty of rainfall will encourage greenery at the expense of the blooms. Trimming the ends of the longest branches will encourage bushiness, and this will also encourage the development of stockier wood. Wild roses should bloom within three years of seeding. Maybe there really are some plants which grow better here than in England. It's an incredible thought.

What varieties of climbing roses do best here? Which honeysuckles?

In George Shewchuk's "Rose Gardening on the Prairies"[28], George explains the difficulties in growing climbers on the prairies which need to be bent down and laid on the ground in the fall before being covered and protected for the winter. He emphasises their need to bloom on second year wood, so it is

28. Shewchuk, George W., Rose Gardening on The Prairies, Faculty of Extension, University of Alberta, Pages 18-19.

very important to assist the wood in overwintering. With this special care, he recommends 'Blaze', 'Danse du Feu', 'Marigold', 'Morning Jewel', and 'Rosarium Uetersen'.

Another rose expert, Don Heimbecker of Calgary, says the genetics of the new shrub roses are so mixed the distinction between shrub and climbing roses has become nebulous - "you can't really separate the two anymore". Heimbecker's 'Morden Centennial' "shrub rose" has reached a height of four metres in the past thirteen years; it looks like a typical climber. While plants sold as climbing shrub roses in the hardy 'Explorer' series include 'Henry Kelsey' and 'John Cabot', he finds the 'John Cabot' the hardier of the two. He takes the stems off their trellis in the fall, places wooden boards over them, and then throws an old rug on top of the whole works to completely cover the stems. The 'John Cabot' blooms for a full three months, and, in Don's opinion, it is an "absolutely, marvellous spreading climber".

A friend of mine, Sue Sanders, grows the old fashioned climber, 'New Dawn', because of sentimental reasons, but doesn't bother training it up an arbour. Instead, she encourages it to branch and form a rambling rose of moderate proportions and delicate pink blooms. She was so convincing in her arguments for this soft pink beauty, I added one to my back yard beside my 'Yellow Rose of Texas' (Harrison's Yellow Shrub Rose) which is not a climber. The advantage to 'New Dawn', stresses Sue, is this climbing rose blooms on new wood, so even though it is not fully top hardy, it will sprout and rebloom each spring.

The only climbing honeysuckle to thrive in northern gardens is the scarlet trumpet honeysuckle, *Lonicera x Brownii* 'Dropmore Scarlet'. It takes a few years to establish, and the rich nectar attracts both hummingbirds and aphids. The flowers range from pale to bright orange.

My double flowering plum is getting very wide, and I love it

Other hardy shrub roses recommended as outstanding, although they are not climbers, include 'Winnipeg Parks', 'Jens Munk' and 'Prairie Dawn'. If you can get the roses on their own root, they will take off faster, and if they do sucker up from the root, the suckers will be the same as the main plant.

so much but want to shape it and make it slimmer. When and how should I do this?

Your flowering plum (*Prunus triloba multiplex*) is worth cherishing. In a good spring, there will be blooms from the base of each branch to the tip. It is a cloud of pink and bumblebees. Because it is a hybrid and flowers are sterile, it rarely produces fruit, but the blooms are worth the space the shrub takes in the garden.

The best time to prune any spring flowering shrub is after it has fully leafed out or by late June. Take the oldest branches out right down to the ground. Leave more than two thirds of the total woody growth during the pruning process. After removing some of the oldest branches (which are easily identified as the widest stems), shorten some of the others to reduce the overall plant size a little; make sure to leave some height variation in the stems for a more natural look. For a beautiful specimen, leave a generous area of at least two and a half metres for each shrub when planning your garden. Then do a small amount of corrective pruning each spring to keep the growth steady and not too rampant. A little tune-up pruning throughout July and August to prevent leggy erratic sprouts will produce a lovely shaped plant worth a special spot in your garden.

Beautiful double flowering plums can be pruned to maintain a smaller shape.

My Mayday has aphids.

My Manitoba maple has aphids.

Any tree (you name it) has aphids.

Aphids will be attracted again and again to the same tree. Initially, the tree is probably stressed, and it telegraphs this stress message to the insect world. Some believe this may be an evolutionary advantage, because a single stressed tree that attracts the bulk of the insect population acts as the "sacrificial lamb" and, in effect, it protects the rest of the forest. Many trees are planted too deep initially, and when this happens, the roots are forced to grow up to get enough oxygen and nutrient.

In other cases, trees receive too much nitrogen because they are grown in heavily fertilized lawns. The root zones of grass and trees are similar so they share the nitrogen. Trees with too much nitrogen attract aphids. Stressed trees may survive this way for many years but they rarely thrive.

A mixture of one cup vegetable cooking oil and one tablespoon dishwashing soap used at a rate of one to two teaspoons per cup of water every ten days will control whiteflies, aphids, and spider mites on small ornamental and vegetable crops.

After stressed trees start to attract insects, they are sprayed with insecticides, and then they suffer even more stress as they react to the sprays. The bottom line is this: look at your trees with aphids in a new way. Are they too deep; too close to a sidewalk or building; underplanted with flowers; cut back incorrectly or too often; sending up water sprouts and suckers; growing in a lawn; oozing sap from weed-eater or insect injury points; or overfertilized with nitrogen? The trouble with trees is that they respond to trouble. Watch your maintenance and tender loving care are not pushing your trees closer to the firewood pile.

Once you have taken a good look at your tree, decide if its conditions can be improved or if it is better removed. If you plan to keep it, start a program of total plant health care which will include limited fertilizing in June; mulching to the drip line or beyond; careful and limited pruning in the correct seasons only; and plenty of water.[29]

Finally, hose the tree down regularly to dislodge any aphids or sap that may be attracting aphids. Using insecticidal soap monthly when the plants are washed down will also help, but if you prefer to wait for the ladybird beetles to move in that's okay too. Leaving leaves on the ground until late in the spring, and tolerating a few aphids will encourage natural populations of ladybird beetles to build up.

---

29. The summer of 1993 saw unprecedented rainfall in the Calgary area which left the impression trees would be suffering. In fact there was no suffering unless the trees were planted incorrectly (with a tree well). This taught us that we probably really do underwater our trees in this prairie town and it has encouraged an upswing in mulching to conserve the rain we do get as well as increased watering across the board. Directing your rain runoff to water barrels or towards high water use trees instead of streets is also an option.

Next winter, just before the buds break in spring, spray your most aphid-infested trees with dormant oil.

Is there any way to get rid of ants?

Ants are a common problem in my south facing front yard. How can I get rid of them?

You have probably unknowingly provided the ideal ant habitat in your warm, sunny front yard. Ants have successful underground colonies only where they can keep their queen and the various chambers dry. In unwatered situations, this often becomes a site under a sidewalk near a sunny south exposure. Although small ant traps are available commercially, this is simply a bandaid solution unless you also take the steps to make the area undesirable for ants. Remember ants can't tolerate long term moisture, so using a soaker hose regularly on sites affected will be a good start.

Pouring boiling water on the known ant nest sites may also have an impact. Unfortunately, the boiling water kills grass as well, so only use this technique in non-turf areas.

I have also encouraged people to use an icing sugar/borax mixture near building foundations that are affected. The old home remedy of borax with icing sugar has been packaged for convenience by several suppliers. It is available with a sticky pad which can be safely attached to the house or other structure for control of ants. It works by attracting the worker ants which gather up the toxic substance and bring it back to the nest where they feed it to the immature insects and the queen. It is sold under the trade name Creepy Crawly Ant Control System.

You can make your own mixture if you can containerize it so that it doesn't wash away each time it rains or when you water. Remember, borax may act as a soil sterilant and will kill soil as well as ants so should be used sparingly. I have heard of cases where large patches of soil have been killed because of overly generous applications of borax. One lady replaced the plants (more than once in a summer) in a spot previously treated with borax with no success.

There are some types of ants not attracted to sugar, so if you find borax and sugar ineffective, you may have ants that prefer fats over sugars. In this case, try mixing a few drops of ant poison in a small amount of pie dough which is of a paste-like consistency.[30] Again, place the poison in a margarine or similar container with little entry holes cut to allow ant access but not rain.

Wood ash sprinkled near foundations will also discourage ants. Once the problem is generally reduced, the planting of ant-repellant plants may help keep it that way. Try pennyroyal or spearmint. Finally, changing the habitat in the garden will discourage ants. If a layer of mulch or area under a building overhang is extremely dry, try installing a leaky pipe system which keeps soils moist without using huge quantities of water or losing much water to the air.

Ants love aphid honeydew, so once again if you minimize nitrogen fertilizer on your trees and shrubs, the aphids will be minimized, as will the ants that follow. Testing is underway to develop strains of *Bacillus thuringensis* lethal to ants. "Bt" is a bacteria known to kill other insects and there are several strains on the market.

How do you divide an iris?

Lift the whole clump of bearded iris a month or more after it has finished blooming. After lifting the iris, roots and all, gently tug apart the rhizomes by hand. Separate the newest parts of root from the older, thicker, and partially decomposing portions. Once the clumps are generally divided, use a sharp clean knife to trim off any broken or damaged ends from the rhizome. Trim back the leaves, and lay the clean trimmed pieces on the lawn in the sun for an hour or so for solar sterilization.

---

30. Ants in the Home, Crop Protection Newsletter, Page 3, Volume 16, Number 7. Alberta Agriculture, ASCHRC, Brooks, Alberta.

Yellow-headed sawflies can disfigure spruce trees. Be careful not to affect the birds feeding on the sawflies when you treat the tree.

What is this bug?

You have yellow-headed sawfly on your spruce tree. You should get rid of it right away before it eats all of the new growth and beyond on your tree. Try soap sprays, natural insecticides containing pyrethrums, or having a spray company come in with insecticides if this is a really big tree. You could ignore sawfly damage. It disfigures the tree and may eventually kill it if there are lots of sawflies, but the reason I know I have sawfly is the first week of July I watch the northern orioles gathering on my spruce, pecking at the branch tips. These beautiful, bright orange birds are welcome in my yard, and when I see them I know the sawflies are back again. I also know I don't want to spray with anything stronger than pyrethrums or soap, and only in the late evening when the birds are not around. Usually I just forfeit my tree to the birds. I only have one spruce, of course, not a whole shelterbelt. I might have to take it a little more seriously if the size of my "crop" was greater.

Would a weed bar work for dandelions?

Yes, if used as directed it will control dandelions, but so does hand digging which will have a lower environmental cost.

How do you control fairy ring in the lawn?

If the lawn is more than five years old it is susceptible to fairy ring which will move in naturally or through infected lawn care equipment or on the soles of your feet. There is no "control" but there is hope. The best approach is to "mask and hide" the damage. (See September for details.)

When does a poplar become unsafe? What size or age?

Age isn't usually a factor in tree safety. Even poplars, which are fairly weak and soft wooded will not necessarily be unsafe with age. It is more likely they are unsafe following unsafe pruning practices. Where a tree has been topped, the strong vertical and lateral support cells are removed, and only a few weak support cells remain on the wild sprouting rank growing branches. These sprouts which result from large flush cuts, or hard cuts made into large branches, are all dangerous and should be prevented by correct pruning. (See February diagrams.)

Remove old trees which have been topped or have a professional arborist thin out the weakest sprouts which will be obvious in the winter. As well, very old branches of any tree will gradually change from pointing straight up, to becoming more lateral, to finally bending down somewhat. Where a tree branch turns and begins to curve down, the branch attachment point is weakened and the whole branch should be removed. Look also for branches which have appeared out of wound sites. They will not be strong and may fall off in winds. Any cracking along the main trunk of a branch or seepage of bacterial ooze will indicate some internal problems and rotting which may indicate trouble. Finally, look for mushrooms in crotches and at the base of trees. If in doubt, call in a professional arborist to have a look at your tree and give a tree health evaluation.

Can we grow Swedish columnar aspen (*Populus tremula erecta*) in Pincher Creek, and where is it available?

Yes, you will be able to grow this hardy tree in any northern garden. It has only one problem. The narrow angle of the branches, which give it a fine upright form, sometimes encourage entry of bacterial or fungal diseases which cause a weak point in the tree. Check the branches on the tree before you buy a young tree to ensure there are no sunken or discoloured portions around the branch bases. These are widely available and easy to obtain from most of the larger nurseries. The best way to ensure success with this or any tree is to start small. Young trees establish themselves much quicker than old ones partly because a higher percentage of the tree is alive and growing, and partly because root damage will be minimal on a small tree as compared to a mature one.

Rose

Lilac

Calendula

Pansy

I would like a list of flowers you can eat.

Several flowers are edible including:

From Trees and Shrubs:

- Apple blossoms
- Elderberry
- Plum
- Rose petals
- Lilac

From Bulbs and Perennials:

- Bergamot *(Monarda* sp.)
- Borage *(Borage officinalis)*
- Chive and other ornamental onions *(Allium* sp.)
- Chrysanthemums & daisies (several genera)
- Dandelion *(Taraxacum officinale)*
- Daylily *(Hemerocallis* cvs.)
- Gladiola *(Gladiolus* cvs.)
- Grape hyacinth *(Muscari* sp.)
- Hollyhock *(Alcea rosea)*
- Johnny Jump Up *(Viola tricolor)*
- Lavender *(Lavendula angustifolia)*
- Pinks *(Dianthus* sp.)
- Red clover *(Trifolium pratense)*
- Violet *(Viola odorata)*

From annual flowers and vegetables and house plants:

- African violet *(Saintpaulia* sp.)
- Annual dianthus *(Dianthus* cvs.)
- Calendula *(Calendula officinalis)*
- Garden pea *(Pisum sativum)*
- Nasturtium *(Tropaeolum* sp.)
- Pansy *(Viola wittrockiana* cvs.)
- Pot marigold (See Calendula)
- Scarlet runner bean *(Phaseolus coccineus)*

- Scented or regular geranium (*Pelargonium* cv.)
- Squash, pumpkin and zucchini

Avoid poisonous flowers such as amaryllis, anemone, azalea, bleeding heart, *Clematis, Datura*, daffodil, delphinium, *Euphorbia*, foxglove, hyacinth, *Hydrangea, Iris*, larkspur, *Lantana*, lily-of-the-valley, lupin, monkshood, oleander, periwinkle, poinsettia, primrose, sweet peas (*Lathyrus* sp.), rhododendron, tansy, and wisteria. If in doubt, call your closest Poison Control Centre which will be in a hospital.

Geranium

I have slugs. They are destroying everything. Some plants, like peas, are starting to look "lacy". What is the latest on how to destroy them?

Well, the really serious slug hunters go out at dusk and again at dawn to hand pick them off their plants. They toss captured slugs in hot soapy water as they are gathered up, or sprinkle salt on the critters they find "on the spot". Real slug fiends hunt by moonlight and flashlight, and even track their numbers as summer progresses with reports of diminishing numbers by early August. Some people even keep chickens so they'll have a use for the collected slugs i.e., chicken feed. A new biological control is in the works which may help us out a lot. The larval stage of fireflies eat eggs and the youngest stages of slugs. The development for this up and coming biological control is slow because the life cycle of fireflies is a full year.[31] There is also some hope for nematode control of slugs which is also promising and worth watching for (See fungus gnat question in January).

Chive

Nasturtium

Slugs (*Limax maximus*) are really just shell-less snails closely related to oysters, clams, and octopuses. They lay eggs in the fall in groups of 30 to 50; the eggs are covered with a yellowish slime which hardens around them.[32] Hunting for and destroying

---

31. Discussions with Applied Bionomics owner Don Elliott. Spring 1994.
32. P 67, Diseases and Pests of Ornamental Plants, Pascal P. Pirone, The New York Botanical Garden. The Ronald Press Company, New York. 4th Edition 1970.

the egg masses by careful cultivation of the soil in the spring is one option.

Here are a number of less ambitious techniques for ridding the garden of this greedy, plant devouring critter:

• *Repel Slugs:* copper gives slugs a jolt and barriers made of copper strips may slow down or stop slugs from reaching your plants. As slugs try to cross the copper stripping, they exude their slime. It causes a chemical reaction which gives the slug an electrical jolt. A copper strip attached to the base of planters works well. This would be expensive if you did it on every pot or planter, but it is a special control for special plants or planters. Strips come with or without an adhesive backing in rolls. A similar product, which is used to set up a barrier around special plants and planters, is the salt-coated vinyl strip sold as "Slug D-fence". It dehydrates slugs as they try to glide across the surface.

• *Discourage Slugs:* scatter wood ashes, crushed eggshells, diatomaceous earth, ground nut shells, roof shingles, or sharp sand around the base of each plant. These items, to varying degrees, discourage slugs or physically cut them so that they die fairly quickly after crawling through the barrier. Diatomaceous earth, for instance, is really just finely powdered prehistoric diatoms which are very sharp. They kill all soft-bodied insects including cabbage loopers. These items will be variously cheap or expensive, depending on what you have on hand, but are worth a try. Top up the barriers after each rainfall, or as materials become available. I particularly like wood ash, because it encourages healthy plant growth by supplying extra potassium.

• *Trap Slugs:* Various slug traps have been offered commercially, and these work as well as the homemade versions. A bait such as beer (especially the cheap, preservative-filled brands) attracts many slugs. The slugs may crawl out again though, so make sure the slug dishes are smooth and are sunk into the ground. This way, the slugs can easily fall in but not as easily climb out. The keen slug killer will need to empty these traps daily.

A version of the basic beer trap is the citrus rind lure. Place grapefruits, eaten-side down, throughout the garden. Each morning, pick them up and kill the slugs captured. The downside is that while grapefruits will attract slugs, they will also decompose quickly in the garden in the summer. I find they last less than a week before they turn to mush and compost themselves on the spot.

Slugs usually hide under boards placed in the garden during the day, so many people place a board in each row and flip it over each morning to scrape off and destroy the offenders.

• *Spray 'Em:* Various solutions have been suggested for killing slugs safely including a 50-50 mixture of water and vinegar.[33] Squirt the offenders with your mixture from a hand spray mister bottle. This may affect the plants over time, so may be best early in the morning followed by picking up of the dead slugs and misting the plants with clear water to prevent "acid rain" symptoms.

Try a solution of ferrous sulphite at a rate of five millilitres to one litre of water sprayed on and around plants.[34] This may burn some plants, so try a few in each row at first to test the effects before you begin. Limit this application to non-edible plantings and do not substitute ferris sulphite for ferrous.

Dried quackgrass is an excellent defence against slugs when sprinkled on the soil around affected plants. Use a small amount only because large quantities of dried quackgrass will be toxic to plants as well as slugs.[35]

---

33. "More on Vinegar-Water Spray for Snails and Slugs", Hortideas, March 1994, 11(3):26.

34. "Iron Sulfate Controls Slugs and Snails", Hortideas, April 1992, 9(4):39.

35. The Avant Gardener, Pg 8, Vol 25, No 1. Nov 1992.

Shrub and Tree Care- A Seasonal Overview

Regardless of where you live, the seasons are the same - only their length varies. While one region may have a longer spring, another surely makes up for it with a longer winter - either way, there are only fifty two weeks in a year and spring always follows winter. Knowing what is happening biologically with your trees and shrubs is more valuable than knowing exactly which week you should prune. Use this guide and follow clues from nature rather than a calender to decide when to do your tree and shrub work!

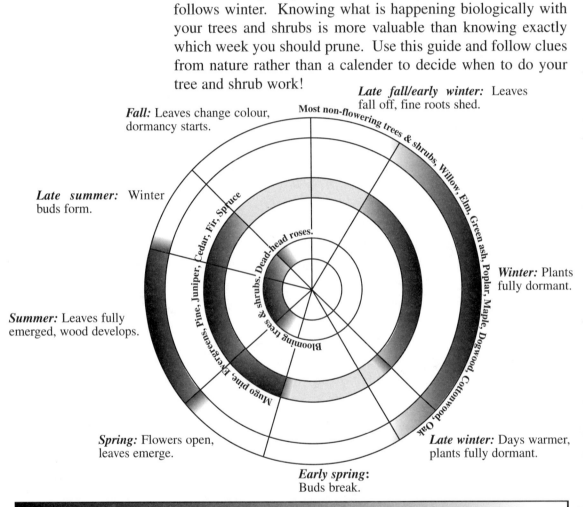

Late fall/early winter: Leaves fall off, fine roots shed.

Most non-flowering trees & shrubs, Willow, Elm, Green ash, Poplar, Maple, Dogwood, Cottonwood, Oak

Fall: Leaves change colour, dormancy starts.

Late summer: Winter buds form.

Evergreens, Pine, Juniper, Cedar, Fir, Spruce

Dead-head roses.

Winter: Plants fully dormant.

Summer: Leaves fully emerged, wood develops.

Mugo pine, Evergreens, Pine, Juniper

Blooming trees & shrubs.

Spring: Flowers open, leaves emerge.

Late winter: Days warmer, plants fully dormant.

Early spring: Buds break.

PRUNE

DON'T PRUNE

Late fall/early winter:

• top growth is dormant but we can't be sure roots are dormant yet (this takes an additional two to six weeks after leaf drop)
• water trees heavily just before they shed their root hairs for winter
• towards end of this period, evergreens may safely be moved

Winter:

• trees and shrubs are dormant
• pruning now will encourage suckering, so if the goal is new growth (i.e., to renew an old shrub or get better winter colour from dogwoods and shrub willows) prune now
• prune elm, maple, poplar, green ash, willow
• avoid pruning any shrub or tree which has early spring blossoms from buds which were carried over the winter - i.e., lilac, bridal wreath or garland spirea, forsythia, camellia, rhododendron, double flowering plum, flowering almond, mountain ash, hawthorn, cherry, apples, Mayday.
• knock off any snow piling up on your evergreen trees
• prune evergreens whenever the wood is not frozen

Late winter:

• ideal time for pruning oak
• trees are still dormant but buds are becoming obvious on some species
• roots are not growing yet
• water woody plants only if soil is bare of snow and very dry to the touch
• prune evergreens whenever the wood is not frozen
• encourage fruit production by removing old raspberry canes which fruited last summer and a few of the oldest (thickest) branches on currant, gooseberry, and saskatoons

Early spring:

• buds break - earliest flowers start to emerge

- roots begin to grow again
- never ever prune at this time of year
- water trees and shrubs if top few inches of soil are dry to the touch
- fertilize only if trees are established (trees planted in the last one to two years will suffer if they get too much nitrogen)

Spring:

- leaves emerge
- don't prune! Candles on pine or new growth on spruce may be pinched to shorten but keep the shears in the cupboard
- water, but make sure water does not sit around the base of trees and shrubs
- plant trees the new way (see diagram in May), mulch them right away, and water them well

Summer:

- leaves are fully emerged
- in a tree's world there are as few as four to six weeks of summer in our northern gardens. This true summer is the period after the leaves are fully emerged and before the buds begin to set for the winter. New annual growth rings are being formed in the tree
- while poorly planted trees with tree wells might suffer in heavy summer rains or from heavy watering, it is almost impossible to water well planted or mature trees too much in the summer. Give them plenty
- summer pruning of spring-blooming shrubs and trees is completed in this brief season
- summer flowering shrubs will bloom more if old blooms are removed (i.e., roses)

Late summer:

- branch tips are still growing, but the main growth for the summer is over now

- heat stress and insect attacks mean trouble for trees, so provide plenty of water and stop pruning!
- don't fertilize
- to kill an unwanted tree, cut it down now, just before the leaves begin to change colour

Fall:

- leaves begin changing colour and falling... stop watering to allow this to begin
- trees store energy in branches and roots for winter
- don't prune any tree or shrub now
- don't transplant any tree or shrub now
- don't fertilize any tree or shrub now

Chapter Seven
J · U · L · Y
The Bugs Bite Back

$\mathcal{G}$ardeners are easy to please. A new flower in bloom as we return from the long weekend is enough to keep us happy a whole day. And then there are the rich shades of green, quickly growing vines to supply a little shelter under a trellis or arbour and the nightly salads of exotic and common lettuce with a touch of "salade mesclun" for flavour.

Trumpet lily (left).

A boost for ordinary salads comes from greens grown for their spicy unusual flavours. Mixtures of greens are often available at grocery stores but are now also available as seed mixes and bedding plants. Ten or more types of greens are included in mesclun mixes which are grown in the garden or in special seedling flats for a few weeks and harvested while they are young. The mesclun mix may contain escarole, dandelion, red and green leaf lettuce, romaine, chervil, parsley, purslane, nasturtium, and more. Buy pre-made mixes or mix your own seed.

In the garden this month, the annuals are beginning to peak as are the lilies. We see our borders of flowers reaching their prime, and our fruit trees begin to set fruit. Spring cares are gone, and the seasoned mid-summer pleasures in the garden are ours to enjoy. 🍃

How do you keep a nice clean edge between the sidewalk and lawn, or especially between a lawn and flower bed?

Either the hard, cheap way, or the expensive, noisy, quick way. The cheap way is with a hand edger available as a hand tool from garden tool suppliers. This should be done at least twice a year and as you edge, make sure the soil line along the turf is clean and sharp with the soft soil tossed well away from the turf edge. If the soft soil piles back against the turf edge, the roots of the lawn will regrow into the space within a few days. The

To Do This Month:
- 🍃 *Dead-heading.*
- 🍃 *Seed collecting.*
- 🍃 *Powdery mildew patrol.*
- 🍃 *Water, water, water.*
- 🍃 *Fertilize trees and shrubs.*

131

Sharp, clean edges really set off a nice lawn or flower garden.

plastic edging widely sold to keep the soil and turf apart is pretty much useless unless it is installed properly with lots of anchor spikes to hold it in place. As well, it must be placed low enough to mow easily over the edge. Without proper anchoring, the edge moves around with winter frosts, the grass grows taller along the plastic edge, and the roots creep beneath the edging to reappear on the soil side.

The fast, expensive way to edge involves a gas edger which allows you to define the edges of your flower beds every few weeks. With a gas edger, you won't need a plastic mowing strip, because the soil will create the edge. One edging machine, the Red Max, is very good. Gas edgers may be for rent at a local equipment rental shop near you. If so, try out different brands to determine which is the right weight and handleability for you.

What is dead-heading, and do you have to do it with all plants?

The process of picking off dead flowers from plants is dead-heading. It keeps the plants looking better, and prevents the spread of diseases which may be carried on dead or dying petals. It is a nice touch in a truly perfect garden, but not absolutely necessary. When you do take the time to dead-head, especially in the case of annual flowers and roses, you will be rewarded with bonus flowers.

I am wondering if you can give me any tips on collecting wildflower seeds from my property for planting next year?

You will have to keep an eye on the seed heads so you don't miss collecting the flowers you want most. Each flower type will mature at its own rate, beginning with the prairie crocus (*Anemone patens*) in late May, and ending with coneflower and *Gaillardia* in September and early October. Plants change drastically in appearance from flowering to maturity which make them hard to recognize once the flowers are gone. Because it is on your own property, you may want to put surveyor's tape on a stake near the plants you want most to allow for easier identification.

Once the flowers fade, the seeds gradually develop. On flowers in the daisy family, wait until the seeds are virtually falling off the plant before you collect seed. Any pulled off the flower head will not be ripe, and will not grow. These include native *Townsendia, Gaillardia, Ratibida* (coneflowers), and erigeron (*Fleabane*). Others, like *Campanula* (bluebells or harebells), will be ripe when the top of the pod opens slightly, and the black, shiny seeds can be shaken out.

Native *Monarda* also has seeds that shake out from dry brown seed heads when ripe. Try shaking a few in the field. If the seeds come out readily, cut a 15-30 centimetre length of flower stalk and put the whole works into a dry paper bag. Leave these to dry an additional couple of weeks in a garage or basement, then separate the seed from the seed heads, and store the seed away in a cool, dry place. A ziplock baggie in the fridge is ideal, but coffee cans, film canisters, or yogurt containers also work.

If possible, scatter the seed where you want it to grow soon after it is harvested. If you want the seed to go further, pot it up in early winter, pop the potted, watered seeds into a plastic bag, and set the whole works outside. When the seed starts to sprout in the spring, take it out of the bag. Or, if you want to force it

Always check with the landowner before collecting "wildflower" seed on their property. To protect the natural wildflower stands, never collect more than 10% of the seed from any one plant or plant group. Always collect from more than a single plant to get the widest possible genetic diversity, and make a note of the collecting location for later follow-up. While direct seeding in the garden does work, special culture indoors or in a greenhouse will yield a higher germination rate, which will make better use of the carefully collected seed.

Don't collect or buy seed from out-of-state or out-of-province areas for naturalizing in your area. This might transfer different genetic features into your native population, and even replace or weaken your own natural genotypes over time.

133

a little early in a greenhouse or under lights, take it in from outside by early March, keep it moist, and remove it from the bag as it germinates. Transplant into flats once the little plants are sturdy enough to move. Keep the plants under bright lights (within 15 centimetres of a fluorescent tube or in a greenhouse). Move plants out to rows in the garden by late May, and transplant to their final spot in the garden the following spring. Most perennials will bloom from seed in the second season.

I am new at gardening, and I am wondering when I can start harvesting potatoes?

Just after the potato plants bloom, the little potatoes will start forming. If you have planted your potatoes on a hill, or in a raised bed, or if you have hilled your potatoes by pulling soil up around the base of the plant, it is possible to scratch the surface of the soil in the raised area and steal a few small potatoes once the blossoms start to fade. Later in the summer it is more practical to pull the entire plant out when you need a few potatoes, but to get the first nuggets of the season scratch around with a small hand-fork or with your fingers.

The leaves on my raspberry bushes are turning yellow. What is happening and how can I control it or stop it?

Researchers in the Netherlands have reported that when pruning or harvesting knives are dipped in sterilized skim milk between cuts, viruses are apparently encapsulated by milk protein and are unable to spread.[36]

There are several virus diseases which become especially noticeable in wet, cool weather. These raspberry diseases are spread by insects, and the symptoms include yellowing and puckering of leaves, as well as dry, shrivelled, seedy fruit. Once a stem or branch of raspberry is diseased, the new stems suckering up from that stem will also be diseased. In other words, all you can do is cut out the stems right at the ground if you see any signs of virus disease. Trash or burn the diseased branches rather than composting them. Ronald J. Howard describes some of the raspberry viruses in his 1993 "Diseases

36. News Briefs, The Avant Gardener, Page 16, Vol. 24, No 2. December 1991.

of Raspberries Special Bulletin".[37]   He recommends cutting back diseased stems as the main control for this type of disease.

There are some really strong tall branches on my raspberry bushes but these strongest branches are not flowering. Why is this?

What do you do about raspberries that aren't in bloom?

The really strong, tall branches are the new "suckers" which have just sprouted since spring. They will not flower or have fruit until next year, which is why it is so important to leave these in place when you prune your raspberries next winter. The stems which bloom this summer should be removed entirely when you prune. The tall, straight, non-flowering branches should be thinned out, but a few left intact for summer fruiting next year.

With raspberries, only second year wood blooms, so the new sprouts that shot up this summer will be the ones that bloom and produce fruit next summer. This is a problem if there has been a harsh winter which kills all the old canes, or if the plants were pruned incorrectly in the winter to remove the newer sprouts while leaving the old. There isn't much you can do about winterkill, but you can identify old branches, which will have small side sprouts on them and won't be as likely to bloom. These may as well be removed in the winter. If you don't allow a large number of this year's sprouts to overwinter, you won't have flowers or fruit next year either.

I want to save tomato seed.

Pick your earliest or sweetest-tasting tomato and squeeze the seed onto a paper towel. In a day or so when the paper towel is dry, put it in an airtight container in a cool spot. It is not too late to save the seed, even if you are in the middle of eating the tomato. If you notice the tomato has great flavour or extra

37. Diseases of Raspberries, Special Bulletin, Ronald J. Howard, ASC & HRC, SS 4, Brooks, AB.

Nasturtiums may flower better in low nitrogen soil if they are in an area of full sun.

sweetness, gather up the remaining seeds onto a piece of paper towel as described. You'll be on your way to developing your own earlier, better breed. Pop the seed in flats next March or early April. Pick the seeds off the towel before seeding.

My nasturtiums are out along my driveway in full sun and they are not blooming yet. Is there anything I can do to encourage them to flower?

Nasturtiums are usually grown from partial shade to full sun; partial shade conditions encourages flowers which are held well above the leaves. In brighter light, the flowers may be tucked underneath the leaves and are not as noticeable. One way to encourage flowers on nasturtiums where the light is bright is to grow these flowers in very poor soil with low nitrogen. The poor soil seems to trigger extra blooms. At this point in the growing season it won't be possible to change the soil or the plant location, so try reducing watering and make sure you don't fertilize with nitrogen. The dry soil may trigger blooms higher on the stems even in your high light location. Some of the newer kinds of nasturtiums like whirlybird and the dwarf jewel series bloom in a wider range of light and soil conditions.

My scarlet runner beans in the greenhouse are not producing "beans" this year. They are flowering well, but the pods are just not forming. I was successful with scarlet runners in the greenhouse before, and even changed the soil last year to make sure there were no nutrient deficiencies. I shake the plants to help with pollination, and there are also plenty of insects in the greenhouse to pollinate. What is happening?

Scarlet runner beans definitely need pollination to set fruit, and the flower shape is complicated, so it is not as easy to pollinate the flowers yourself as it is with tomatoes (which just need a gentle tapping). There are a few possible explanations for your lack of success:

• High temperatures (over 32 degrees Celsius), especially if the air is very dry, will reduce pollination success. If possible, place a high/low thermometer in your greenhouse to monitor temperatures.

• If there is very low humidity combined with dry soil, it is possible the blossoms will drop before they have a chance to be pollinated. Again, possibly add drip irrigation to prevent soil moisture fluctuations.

• Try a new source of seed or a new cultivar if the one you are using refuses to set seed. Who knows, you could have purchased a hybrid. Most hybrids will not set fruit under any conditions.

My hybrid T roses didn't bud this year. They used to bud.

Assuming the original roses are still alive, and not winter killed and regrown from below the graft, they have probably stopped flowering because of decreasing organic matter in the soil. Hybrid T's need a lot of organic matter, and, over the years, this goes downhill remarkably. Top-dressing the beds every summer with an inch or so of composted manure is the best solution, unless you are willing to physically dig out and replace the soil every five to ten years. If a rose is a hybrid, it will have five leaflets in each leaf; if it has suckered from below the graft, it will have seven leaflets. Avoiding the hybrid T's and buying only hardy shrub roses grown on their own roots, will eliminate this trouble.

I have two currant bushes planted quite close together. They always develop a severe case of mildew. Do I need two bushes relatively close together for pollination, or can I move one and improve the ventilation and thus the mildew problem?

Sphaerotheca macularis causes powdery mildew on gooseberry and currant bushes. You probably have alpine currants, which are extremely susceptible to this disease. You don't need two shrubs to get good pollination with this type of shrub, so you are free to move one. A good mixture to counteract powdery mildew is a combination of common household products. See the next question for several alternatives.

My roses and pea plants have a white powdery substance on the leaves. What is this? Is it harmful? And, if it is a problem, how do I get rid of it?

You have classic symptoms of powdery mildew, a fungus disease of plants in the *Ascomycetes* class. It becomes more obvious in cool, damp weather, especially when nitrogen levels are high. At first, the leaves have a white, powdery look to them, which may even look like a light dusting of flour. Eventually the leaves curl, shrivel, and finally drop off the plant. Several trees, shrubs, and other garden plants are affected by the many kinds of powdery mildew. Peas are naturally high in nitrogen because they can "fix" their own as needed; this makes them particularly susceptible. Roses are also susceptible because they are notoriously high "feeders" requiring lots of nitrogen rich organic matter; they may be overwatered and overfertilized quite easily as part of the high level of maintenance they need to produce the expected high number of flowers each season.

Where plants are watered late in the day, or when rain is persistent enough to keep leaves of peas, roses, and other plants moist continuously, powdery mildew is a problem. These powdery mildew fungi don't usually kill the plants they live on, but they may make them look ugly. Try changing your watering and fertilizing habits if that is a problem, and make sure to clean up all fallen leaves. The fungus overwinters and spreads from year to year on dead leaves. There is a non-chemical mixture worth trying if you have this problem which has been recommended for its effectiveness against fungus diseases.

One recommended recipe suggests combining 25 millilitres (five teaspoons) of baking soda with 4.54 litres of water (one gallon)

and mixing this with equal parts of a product called summer oil (i.e., Sunspray).[38]

Another recipe, listed in George Shewchuck's "Rose Gardening on the Prairies", suggests weekly spraying in the summer with a mixture of six millilitres baking soda per litre of water mixed with a spreader/sticker to control both blackspot disease and mildew.

Finally, studies at Cornell University[39] showed that spraying with both baking soda and oil provided the best control of powdery mildew. The plants were sprayed weekly with plain water, a solution of baking soda (about one tablespoon per gallon of water), a 1% solution of "Sunspray" horticultural oil in water, or a solution of both baking soda and oil in water (same concentrations as when applied separately). To control blackspot, baking soda (about one tablespoon per gallon of water) mixed with a small amount of a spreader/sticker ("Tween 20") controlled blackspot better than mixtures with oil. Sunspray is an American summer oil product which is not registered in Canada. Similar studies repeated for control of powdery mildew on lilac indicate plain oil and water mixtures worked best among solutions including baking soda, oil, and insecticidal soap.[40] Two millilitres of oil per 100 millilitres water was the concentration most often cited in studies of oil as a fungus deterrent.

Organic gardeners, who may object to the use of petroleum

38. Fungicide Formula, The Growing Edge, 4(3):71 Spring 1993. The product recommended, Sunspray, is a trade name for a summer oil product which is only available in the United States. We do have Dormant Oil products available in Canada which are very light mineral oils. If mixing a formula for your own home use, it might be worth trying any light oil - such as Canola Oil - to see if you get satisfactory results.

39. "Effect of Sodium Bicarbonate and Oils on the Control of Powdery Mildew and Black Spot of Roses", R.K. Horst (Dept. of Plant Pathology, Cornell University), S.O. Kawamoto, and L.L. Porter. Plant Disease, 76(3), April, 1992, 247-251.

40. Alternatives for Powdery Mildew Control, by David L. Clement, Stanton A. Gill and William Potts, Journal of Arboriculture, 20(4):July 1994.

Various recipes have been proposed to eliminate powdery mildew and blackspot.

based oils, may experiment with vegetable oils (mixed to 2% concentration by volume).[41]

Although it may seem safer to use soaps, oils, and baking soda than chemicals in the home garden, be careful when using oils and oil-based products on green plants. Studies have shown damage to evergreens with summer oils; green plants may suffer if the temperatures are below four degrees Celsius or above 32 degrees Celsius, or if the foliage is wet when summer oils are used. Also, many people assume household detergents are safe. In fact, many detergents are corrosive, and even carry WHMIS labels to that effect.[42]

One final note on roses and mildew: roses need 80% or more direct sun to grow their best. In shadier conditions they are more likely to develop diseases like powdery mildew. Some types of roses are just more susceptible than others to this disease, so check the tag first, or look up the rose you are thinking of buying to see if it is mildew resistant. Or if you refuse to tolerate this disease at all, try rose grower Don Heimbecker's solution to mildew. He throws any affected plants away and orders new cultivars in the spring! Don tells me he hasn't used a pesticide or fungicide in seven years. He simply eliminates any roses which get blackspot in the summer (he has a little sympathy for fall-occurring blackspot because the cool weather contributes). He also rogues out all plants suffering from powdery mildew. A total of two dozen roses a year which have disease or haven't met with his bloom expectations are rogued. Finally, he chooses from among the 40 or 50 new cultivars released each year to find replacements and continue the testing in his garden.

41. "Horticultural Oil: Still Almost Miraculous", Hortideas, January 1994, 11(1):4.
42. WHMIS stands for Workplace Hazardous Materials Information System. All products sold in commercial quantities carry a WHMIS label, and soaps have symbols for both chronic and corrosive principals. Also, soaps and detergents are not the same thing. Tide is a detergent; Ivory Snow is a soap.

My petunias are turning brown and drying up. This has not happened before. Is it the lousy weather?

Look carefully at the base of the plants. It could be that you have a fungus disease affecting plants placed too close together, especially if disease was present in the soil from a previous summer. Once the sclerotinia fungus is in the soil, it is hard to eliminate. Of course, you could always pull the plants out, place them further apart next year, or replant the area with shrubs or perennials. It might, however, be smart to look at the base of the plants first to confirm if you have this disease.

The "resting" bodies or sclerotia are the dormant overwintering stage of this fungus disease, and they look like mouse droppings which are five to ten millimetres long, one to two millimetres wide, and are dark brown in colour. The base of the stems of affected plants will break apart easily, and these little resting bodies will fall out.

Overhead watering or seasons with a lot of "lousy" (i.e., rainy cool) weather encourage the spread of this disease. Some work in the field has indicated the use of a soil additive like Hydrogel (which keeps the soil more evenly moist so allows you to water less frequently) may discourage the spread of this disease.[43] Fungicides are not practical for home use, and the only real solution is as mentioned above unless you want to leave annual flowers out of your planting plan for three to five years once the disease is spotted.

The leaves on my mountain ash are getting smaller and yellow. Some are only yellow between the veins. This has happened before and I am wondering how I can prevent it.

The more you use compost as a soil additive the less problem you are likely to have with fungi.

43. Discussions with Calgary Zoo Ornamentals gardener Sanna V. Barlem have indicated that the Hydrogel trialed on an experimental basis in beds known to carry sclerotinia showed decreased disease even in the rainy summer of 1993. Because sclerotinia persists in the soil for several years, Sanna has chosen to use hydrogel and to space flowers further apart instead of spraying fungicides in the public gardens at the Calgary Zoo.

It sounds like you have classical "lime induced chlorosis", also sometimes called iron chlorosis. This isn't necessarily because of an iron deficiency, and iron fertilizers won't necessarily clear up the problem. The whole thing relates to your soil, the hardiness of the plant roots, and the location of the plant. If the soil pH is above six-and-a-half, the iron could be bound up, and will not be available to the plant as readily. Acidify the soil with additions of peat moss, compost, or sulphur-containing fertilizers.

Sometimes, if we get a lot of rain, or if water is sitting at the base of the tree for any reason, we will see these same symptoms. Really, it is best to try to acidify the soil over the long run and to improve the tree's drainage. In the short term, try using a product called Iron Chelate. It is available from the garden centres. It quickly relieves the visual and minor iron deficiency symptoms on small garden plants, but may be slower in providing relief if the tree is large, or if the problems are related to the roots such as winterkill or overly wet soil conditions.

Extreme cases of these iron-absent symptoms on roses may lead to far more damage than a little paleness between the veins. Many rugosa roses are very touchy about wet feet. When the soil is overly wet, and even if the pH is not high, they show these symptoms by late June or early July. Symptoms are worse if they are planted in a level bed, or even worse if they are planted at the bottom of a sloping bed. The roots simply can't tolerate sitting in water. After the initial paleness, the edges of the rose leaves start to brown and dry like crispy, scorched potato chips. This is just an extreme extension of the same problem.

Roses are susceptible to leaf diseases.

142

It is unusual to see an otherwise hardy shrub rose like 'David Thompson' or 'Henry Hudson' showing these iron deficiency symptoms when it is grown in a good loam with great drainage right beside healthy looking, unaffected 'Winnipeg Parks' and 'John Franklin' shrub roses. The coarser looking rugosa roses like 'David Thompson' and 'Henry Hudson' do seem to be more susceptible to this problem. Other shrub roses likely to show these same leaf-yellowing symptoms include 'Blanc de Coubert' and 'Hansa'.

Either toss out affected plants; move them to a slightly sloping site where there is excellent drainage; try the chelated iron; or change the pH of the soil by using compost which is acidic. Adding fertilizers which contain sulphur and are listed as acidifying the soil may also help.

Some references imply these leaf symptoms are caused by damage to the roots over the winter. If surface roots are damaged because of sitting water which freezes and thaws, or due to extreme dryness over winter, the effect may be similar to iron-induced chlorosis except the addition of iron chelates will not solve the problem. Prevent root damage by mulching your trees and shrubs year round wherever possible.

I have what looks like slugs on my rose leaves, and on my hawthorns. What are they?

You have pear slugs, also known as pear sawflies because they are really the larval stage of a small black sawfly (*Caliroa cerasi*). These slimy, soft-bodied, immature animals rasp away the top surface of the leaves on many trees and shrubs including the ones you have mentioned as well as cotoneaster hedges. The final effect is a plant with leaves that have dry, brown, skeletonized patches. Hosing off the leaves with a soapy solution will work if the stream of water is strong and the shrub small. Using products containing diatomaceous earth - fossilized diatoms - may also work if the plant is small and if you can get good coverage. Hand picking is also a possibility. Obviously, because the larval stage is so obvious and soft-bodied, it will be very fragile and easily killed with all sorts of products. The vinegar and water solution recommended for garden slugs may also work here but make sure to test it on a few leaves first. The acidic vinegar could damage the leaves and leave you with "acid rain" symptoms on the leaves. Whatever treatment you use, just make sure you aim your attentions on the insect and not the already dead leaves. In other words, learn more about the life cycle of this pest.

Pear slugs start as an egg laid on the lower leaf surfaces of all plants in the cherry/rose family (*Rosaceae*) between mid-June and mid-July. After a few weeks, the eggs hatch and the small larvae, which look like tiny tadpoles, crawl to the upper side of the leaf to feed. When they are full grown, they are about a centimetre long, and by this time the leaves of the affected plants are covered with scabby patches which may have a reddish tint. The tree often sheds the affected leaves, so by late August, it appears the tree or shrub is already going dormant for fall. There won't be any long term damage to plants having pear slugs, but it is unsightly and who wants their trees to be losing leaves in August? The mature larvae drop to the ground once they are full size, and spin a cocoon. There may be a second generation before winter, or the pupae may remain in the soil until spring when the small black sawflies emerge to reinfect the same or neighbouring trees.

Look carefully at plants affected by pear slugs earlier in the summer next year. If you can control the first generation, there won't be a second, and more damaging generation.

There are some weird pinecone-like growths forming on my willow. What is this from? Is it normal?

There are all kinds of insects and mites that cause galls on willow and poplars, but the type of gall you have described is a

Remove and throw away these pinecone-like galls to control the midges.

sign of willow pinecone gall midge (*Rhabdophaga salicis-batatas*). Luckily this little midge only has one generation per year, and the third phase of its life (third instar) overwinters within the pinecone looking gall. The adult midges will emerge from this gall in the spring just before the willow leafs out. If you remove these galls as soon as you see them, and especially if you see them in the winter, you will effectively remove all the midges on your willows! This is the easiest form of control known for any insect. Sharpen your shears and get to it! Remember to burn or garbage the removed galls because dropping to the ground or in the compost will allow the midge to finish its development, and go on to reinfect the tree in the spring.

Also, if you miss removing these galls, the females will mate in the spring and go on to lay eggs singly on the small, emerging leaves. The feeding of the young larvae on the leaf causes the galls to form.

What is this hard black stuff on my Mayday tree?

Black knot of cherry, which is caused by *Apiosporina morbosa* (also known as *Dibotryon morbosum*) is in the *Ascomycetes* group of fungus. These really noticeable and easily recognized black swellings are seen on favourite landscape trees in the cherry group such as Mayday, plum, chokecherry, and pin cherry. It is especially common on trees leading a stressed life. Soft green, velvet-like swellings occur on the branch or trunk of the affected tree in the spring and by fall, they turn black. It often isn't noticed at all until winter, when the leafless stems look odd with their black swellings, so it is possible to buy trees with this disease and not even notice it.

The swellings will increase in size each year as the disease continues, so the best control is to remove affected branches as soon as you see the damage. Make sure to make cuts 10 cm below the "black knot" to eliminate all of the fungus. Burn

These black swellings are easily detected in the winter on trees such as Maydays.

145

or trash the removed parts, and clean your shears with a bleach solution between each cut.

Now, have a closer look at that tree. Are you doing anything to put it into such stress that it is subject to these fungal attacks? Just asking.

Is there a difference between Engelman ivy and Virginia creeper?

Yes. Engelman ivy (*Parthenocissus quinquefolia* 'Engelmannii') is a form of Virginia creeper *(Parthenocissus quinquefolia)*. The Engelman ivy is listed in Hortus III as having leaflets slightly smaller than the Virginia creeper.[44] The Engelman form is also distinctive because it has suction-pad style tendrils which actually stick to building surfaces, and may cause some damage to the building. The hardiest form of the two is the plain Virginia creeper, but there is a lot of variation even within this species. If you manage to get a piece established, propagate it by covering a piece of vine with soil in the fall, and digging the rooted cutting in the spring. As well, if you have a friend with a hardy Virginia creeper which has good fall colour and does not get powdery mildew (a common problem on these vines), propagate a piece of their vine instead of buying it.

My Nanking cherry (*Prunus tomentosa*) has red spots on the branches. What is this and what can be done about it?

You have *Nectria*, also known as coral spot on your cherry. This is also quite common on cotoneaster (*Cotoneaster lucidus*) hedges, especially on older branches of older hedges. *Nectria* is a decay fungus which shows up on dead and dying branches, and is a sign of aging in shrubbery. Simply prune out the oldest branches of a shrub in the early summer or, if you prefer pruning in mid-winter, you'll remove some of the blossoms. Prune to remove the oldest stems and encourage

44. Hortus III, A Concise Dictionary of Plants cultivated in The United States and Canada, L. H. Bailey & E. Z. Bailey, MacMillan Publishing Company, New York.

younger, disease-free growth. Coral spot doesn't do much damage because it is a sign of decay rather than a killer fungus. It is good to take the cue from nature and do the necessary thinning.

My hibiscus needs water every second day. What should I do?

When a houseplant needs water more than once a week, this is your cue to transplant it into a bigger pot. Don't move up more than one pot size at a time. If you want to keep the plant small, leave it alone, and settle with watering it as often as it requires.

Chapter Eight
A·U·G·U·S·T

Official Hammock Season

*E*very year I equate August with hammock season. All the spring and summer work is done, the plants are maturing nicely, and the gardener's reward is a few hours a day worth of sketching or daydreaming from the hammock. The reality may be climactic disaster, unprecedented waves of winged aphids arriving on your deck, worms creating havoc in your nicely maturing carrots, late bouts of powdery mildew, or worst of all, bumper crops of only a single veggie leading to massive revolt from your family when zucchini is served every course in a four course meal. "How do you like the Chocolate <u>Surprise</u> Cake, dear?"

Even with the potential for trouble in the August garden, the pros outweigh the cons. Imagine season weary delphiniums bowing from the weight of their outstanding blue spires while hummingbirds nip by to sip their nectar? Or consider lilies in their glory offering their rain glistening petals up for inspection, daisies on the rebloom; lush multi-layered shades of green, reminiscent of tropical vistas; or birds chattering noisily among themselves as they gorge on ripening berries and seed pods.

August is perfect hammock season, as long as your hammock is in a weather-proof, protected location. Let others charge out for back to school supplies or farmer's market rations. You can stay home and dream of new ways to combine your forecasted or real bumper crops of tomatoes, zucchini, and parsnips. This is gardener payback season. It's time to host a get-together to show off your season's efforts, or drop by a friend's with a bouquet of fresh picked flowers or armloads of zucchini. It's August. 🍃

How do I get my pansies to spread out more rather than growing straight up?

Give them a cooler, shadier spot. Pansies tend to bolt when in a warm site, or if the summer temperatures become too intense. They are used in warmer climates as a winter crop, and have

To Do This Month:

🍃*Deadhead annuals to encourage continuous bloom.*

🍃*Remove unwanted suckers from the base of trees by the first week of August.*

🍃*Mix up a batch of soap, water, and oil to effectively minimize annoying aphids.*

🍃*Make a fresh flower wreath for drying.*

🍃*Press tiny lobelia flowers or pea tendrils for fall card making and candle decorating.*

🍃*Analyse the garden to make sure you have plenty of late season bloom from your perennials.*

🍃*Visit garden open houses or public and private gardens to get late season bloom ideas and inspiration.*

🍃*Veggie harvest begins.*

🍃*Slow down watering; let plants start to toughen up for fall.*

occasionally been planted in northern gardens as early as mid-April to capture ideal pansy weather which is under 15 degrees Celsius. A few of the newer cultivars including the bingo series survive summer heat better and won't stretch out as much. Give these newer types a try. There are also several nearly winter-hardy types of pansies worth trying.[45] Clipping off old flowers (dead-heading) sometimes encourages side branching and more flowers in the fall.

I have corky looking marks on my potatoes. My friend has called them scabs. What can I do and are they harmful if eaten?

Scabs are a disease on the surface of the potato skin only. The disease becomes a problem in soils where manures have been used, or where potatoes have been planted too many years in the same spot. Red and other thin skinned types of potatoes are more susceptible to scab than the thicker skinned white potatoes. Scab, except in extreme cases, will not enter the actual potato; it will be removed when the potatoes are peeled. It does not affect the flavour but will affect the length of

Potato scabs do not affect flavour, but they will shorten the storage time.

45. Fall planted pansies or pansies left in after a healthy season of summer growth will often overwinter and rebound in bloom the following April and May. The Winter Wonderland, Crystal Bowl and Regal types are especially good for this. They will not overwinter in every location, but when they do it is a wonderful sight to see the following spring.

storage because scabby potatoes rot quickly when stored.

I am interested in weeping plants and wonder which ones are recommended as hardy and worth trying in a small garden?

Weeping plants, usually trees or shrubs, are like expensive artwork. You wouldn't hang your most expensive painting in the bathroom, and likewise you shouldn't casually place a weeping plant in just any location. Set it in a focal point where the unique form and interesting attitude of the weeping plant can be admired. Weepers add an expensive finishing touch to the garden and are planted for their form, and as a curiosity, rather than for their hardiness. Many are grafted so they will not be long lived in the garden. To ensure success, place them in a protected, well sheltered spot in the garden where they are out of the wind and direct south sun.

Make sure, as well, that weeping plants are placed where they are not likely to be used as a bird roost and where they will not compete with other features for attention. A weeping plant near a bird bath, for instance, is poorly placed. Birds will rest on the plant's fragile (often grafted) branches, and the view of two features, the bird bath and weeping plant, will be distracting and confusing. Instead, place your weeper in a carpet of juniper groundcover or in front of an evergreen tree.

After planting, carefully mulch below the weeping plant with a contrasting or complimentary material. The mulch will help the fairly fragile plant establish. Many dwarf weeping plants are suited to small condominium or infill gardens, and some have been used successfully at the top of rock gardens. Some examples include:

• Weeping larch (*Larix pendula* graft): This non-evergreen conifer sprouts fresh green leaves each spring along its cascading branches. It is a borderline hardy plant which will not grow any taller than its original height because of the placement of the graft. Consider this when purchasing, and make sure to place this fairly small plant where it can be appreciated, near a deck or front entrance. It will be visually lost if tucked within a mature shrub bed or forest of background trees.

• Weeping caragana (*Caragana* hybrids): Both the coarse-leaved "farm style" *Caragana arborescens* and the finer leaved *Caragana walkerii* have been grafted on hardy standards to form miniature, extremely hardy, weeping trees. Both have pale green leaves which contrast nicely with the darker, purple leaf plum (*Prunus cistena*) or evergreens such as blue spruce (*Picea pungens*). They can tolerate some dryness so may be more useful in a south exposure than other weeping shrubs.

• Tolleson's weeping juniper (*Juniperus* 'Tolleson's Weeping'): This is not a grafted plant, but an upright form of juniper with side branches that droop. These have received mixed reviews. First, they need a semi-shaded but not deeply shaded spot. Their growth may appear dead during the winter or, in fact, it may be dead. It is a large shrub which reaches a width of two metres with a height of five metres. The leaves are a silvery blue, and, once established, it may look fine. Make sure there is an excellent contrast nearby for winter effect such as golden or coral twigged dogwoods (*Cornus flavirama* or *Cornus alba sibirica*)

• Young's weeping birch *(Betula pendula* 'Youngii'): Unlike the other weeping plants mentioned, this one is a giant. It needs an estate property or farm yard to do it justice. It is best portrayed spilling into a massive lake across a broad vista, or in front of a large planting of evergreens for winter effect. The trouble with this tree is it will only grow upwards as long as it is staked. Once the stake is removed, the tree stops gaining height and begins to droop. If the overall height is too short, the branches will then sprawl out and ramble over the ground. Allow this tree to get at least five metres tall before removing the staking. It will eventually get as wide as it is tall. This weeping birch is susceptible to all the same diseases as other birch trees. It definitely benefits from, and looks best with, mulching because the drooping branches and leaves will eventually form a dense shady canopy which won't allow growth of any kind beneath it.

What plants or flowers will grow in acidic soil which tends to be around and under spruce, pine or other evergreen trees?

Don't do it! Don't grow plants immediately under your evergreens. They have set out this hostile protection zone on purpose. Their roots are shallow, and to bring in the moisture needed to keep millions of evergreen needles (leaves) on the payroll, they need all the moisture and root space they can get. This is why they protect their root zone by acidifying the soil and filling the space with roots of their own to make the zone both dry and acidic. Although estimates vary depending on the expert consulted, many tree people agree the roots of evergreens extend at least to the drip line (outside edge of the branches); some researchers believe the roots go another 50% further than the dripline.[46] Protect as big a space as possible under your trees.

During the hottest days of summer plants may go dormant. Extreme heat will shut down activity in trees and plants so make sure to avoid activities that require a plant response: stop fertilizing, pruning, or spraying when temperatures are over 30 degrees Celsius. Mist plants in the early part of the day and water as much as possible to help them get over the stress of high heat conditions.

Does this mean you have to look at the dry brown soil beneath these monumental trees? No! Feel free to decorate with inert materials. Really huge trees suit a garden bench, a lightly used mulch path, or some large boulders under-decorated with smaller rocks such as well rounded river rock or smaller scale pea gravel. Redwood bark chips or woodchips found locally will also suit the site and enhance tree growth by further protecting the rooting zone. Just beyond the drip line you may attempt the always excellent, extremely hardy perennials such as the

46. Root System Care, Gary W. Watson., December 1993, Continuing Education Unit, ISA Bulletin.

153

I was told, and I had also presumed, the soil under a large planting of spruce trees was going to be acidic. I was thinking of planting and soil-fixing alternatives because it was a very large site and far too barren for the owners to tolerate. Before I did anything else, I did a quick pH test and got a real shock. The soil was basic, not acidic! People had been trying for years to "cure" the acidic soil and they had succeeded. The soil pH had become so high, nothing would grow, and acidic peat had to be added to start to counter the effect of assumptions gone wrong.

snow-in-summer mentioned earlier. Astilbe, which is a lovely, late-blooming perennial recommended for all sites across Canada, will thrive with the shade and soil conditions of the tree's dripline if given extra moisture. It blooms in various colours including cream, white, pink, and red. Spent flowers may be removed and used in dry flower arrangements or left on past fall for winter interest.

Do you have any literature on wildflowers and perennials ?

Yes, here it is:

Every plant growing wild which is not a tree, a shrub, a grass, a sedge, a water plant or an introduced weed is a wildflower. This seems so simple it's hard to believe it so often gets mixed up in the press and by seed companies.

"Wildflower" seed mixes, for instance, are wild in what area? The packages never say. Perhaps they are wild to the province or state where the seeds are packaged? This is not always true of "commercial" seeds available in Alberta. Nor is it true anywhere across Canada. The word "wildflower" has marketing appeal, so this designation is often used for seed mixes of annual and perennial plants. I've seen wildflower mixes sold locally which contain the California poppy... a wildflower of California certainly, but I wouldn't class it as a wildflower anywhere else. Real wildflower mixes should contain just the native plants in your area. Here's where it gets sticky. People are geographic splitters or geographic lumpers. If a plant is native to Alberta, should it be sold in Calgary as a wildflower? Possibly, but it might not grow in Calgary if, for instance, it is a native pitcher plant found wild only in Alberta's far northwest corner (an extreme example to be sure!). So, depending on your own viewpoint, you may classify plants found in a region near yours (regardless of province or state) to be "wildflowers" or you may only consider the plants in your nearest local wild park to be wildflowers.

In other words, when considering growing wildflowers, try to identify what it is you want. If you really only want a nice, casual looking, mixed perennial bed, you may be better off selecting the plants individually to achieve the range of colour and season of bloom you want. If you want to let your lawn "go wild" by replacing it with wildflowers, perhaps what you really want is to create Calgary's historic prairie past. In this case, it is better to find actual Calgary grassland natives (unless you live along the riverbanks and prefer to simulate a riverside Riparian habitat). The best references to determine what is really native in your area are the local naturalists' field guides. In Calgary, the Calgary Field Naturalists' species list of plants identified in Calgary parks is an excellent start. In other cities and provinces, contact your local field naturalist group or native plant council. These groups will be able to give you the "ideal" list of wildflowers in your area, and may also have growing suggestions.

There is a trend now among small nurseries to produce native wildflowers in four inch (ten centimetre) pots. Again, if it is wildflowers you want, check with the groups mentioned above and get species lists for the habitat regions in your area. Bring these lists with you when you go shopping and assemble plants to suit your site. It doesn't hurt to try assembling a collection of plants that suit your yard rather than using strictly natives. If you have a bright, full sun back yard, why not recreate the prairie? If your inner city lot is shady and cool you may be better reproducing a mountain stream with native bog and forest understory wildflowers. A successful "wildflower" garden is not going to contain alpine plants from the Rockies in combination with tall-grass prairie plants from the Winnipeg area. It just won't read well, it will be lots of work to maintain, and will be like wearing your Bermuda shorts with a touque - out of sync.

I love wildflowers but I am not convinced the only way to garden is entirely with our natives which can easily be viewed in the larger context of their habitat by going for a stroll in a provincial or national park. For now, I use a few of my favourite native wildflowers, which I have started from seed, as part of a larger perennial flower border and enjoy them as individuals rather than trying to simulate an actual chunk of their habitat. The botanical gardens are already doing that.

One further warning if you are contemplating wildflower mixes. The provincial weed specialists often encounter illegal and noxious weeds in these mixes. While it is not illegal to bring the seeds into one province or another across Canada, once it is growing, the provincial weed specialists have the right to ask you to remove it if the plant is noxious or prohibited. It's unbelievable seeds of this nature are even included in mixes, but even weeds have pretty flowers sometimes, and the risk is there to unconsciously spread the nasties. Our weed inspectors are really looking out for all of us. For lists of weeds considered noxious in your province, contact an agricultural fieldman in your closest county.

Can you suggest a chemical for killing aphids which is not harmful? Presently, I am using commercially available chemicals but would like to change to something which is not as poisonous.

Great! I am happy to hear you are looking at alternatives to insecticides. Unfortunately, by this time of year, many of the aphids are growing wings and will fly off to new sites as you approach with a spray solution. Also, it is always best to look at the whole picture. As mentioned earlier, trees and shrubs under stress actually attract insect pests. If you have ruled this out, try some limited pruning of the infected branches and immediately destroy these branches. Then begin regular hosing of the actual shrubs and trees or be patient and wait for the predators such as ladybird beetles.

Using a soap and oil mixture is a new twist to the old soap solutions we've all tried. Mix one teaspoon (five millilitres)

Safer's Soap with one cup (250 millilitres) vegetable oil and then use two tablespoons (ten millilitres) of this mixture in one cup of water for effective whitefly and insect control.[47] Repeat as needed (approximately every two weeks), preferably in the evening so you are not affecting honeybees or beneficial insects such as ladybugs who may be helping you out by eating your problem. Some detergents such as Ivory dish soap have a degreaser additive which has been shown to harm plant leaves. To be on the safe side, I would always use Safer's Insecticidal Soap in lieu of dish soap when experimenting with this new form of aphid and whitefly control.

Once you try this more sensitive approach, look for signs of success. If you see ladybugs or their larvae, which look like mini black alligators with red spots, you know you are on the way to success. Also, if you see individual aphids which are brown and puffy, like a puffed up balloon, you have attracted a parasite which will help you out of this problem as well. The parasite native to the prairies which causes this symptom on aphids is a braconid wasp.[48] If the aphid mummies still contain

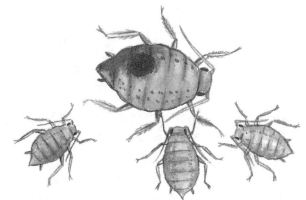

47. "Keeping the Garden Clean", J. DeQuattro, Agricultural Research, Superintendent of Documents, P.O. Box 371954, Pittsburgh, PA, 15250-7954. Volume 40(11):12 November 1992.

48. Steiner, M.Y. and D.P. Elliott, Biological Pest Management for Interior Plantscapes, Vegreville, AB. Alberta Environmental Centre. 30p. 1983. AECV83-E1.

Aphid mummies (top) can be moved to help other plants with aphid problems.

the little parasites, the branch with the mummies attached may be moved to other plants with an aphid problem indoors or out. Use a magnifying glass to see if there is an exit hole in the mummies. If the exit holes aren't there, the parasites still are. This may be the easiest way to kill aphids I have ever discovered.

"To date University of California Researchers have found that ladybugs (*Hippodamia convergens*) leave within a few days following release, regardless of whether they have been released directly from cold storage, warmed and fed honey-water for a week, released in a screened tent for a week, fed honey-water and aphids for a week, or sprayed with flat soda (which has been recommended by some ladybug sellers)."[49]

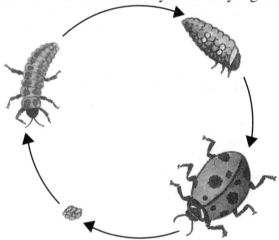

I would like to inquire about hardy lilies. One particular variety of interest we have seen is 'Star Gazer'.

Prairie hardy lilies fall into a few categories, including the hardiest types which are Asiatic hybrids, and the less hardy martagons and Orientals. 'Star Gazer' is an Oriental lily, which means it is not as hardy on the prairies, and goes downhill

Ladybug life cycle clockwise: eggs, larva, pupa, adult.

49. Jill Renter, Mary Louise Flint, Steve Dreistadt, Norman Gary, and Michael P. Parrella. "Lady Beetlemania: Fan or Foe", Greenhouse Grower, 12(2), February 1994, 26-28, 30.

gradually with severe winters. It is a late bloomer, which is probably why it caught your interest late in the season. Another bonus of 'Star Gazer' is its strong beautiful scent.

The hardy Asiatic lilies are bred by several growers right here in Canada. (See Sources). They are also commonly available from Holland in the spring. Spring-available bulbs have been prechilled for the home gardener. They are more expensive than fall-bought, locally grown bulbs, but may appease spring fever better.

Lilies (clockwise from top): Oriental, martagon, trumpet, and Asiatic.

Carlovirus damage

Millipede damage

Normal lily

Trouble With Lilies:

• Lily virus, such as the one in the Carlovirus group, have rather beautiful symptoms initially. The leaves appear pale, especially between the veins; they are also twisted and curled downward. In the first year, flower quality is not affected but the plants quickly go downhill after that and all plants with these symptoms should be removed as soon as damage is noticed because the virus is spread through sap and the feeding of aphids.

• As unusual as it seems, these lilies were damaged by immature millipedes. In soils high in organic matter, the milli-pedes reproduced like crazy and soon went beyond eating dead and decomposing organic matter right into eating living lily bulbs. The symptoms resemble other types of root damage. The leaf tips get brown and dry, and the bottom of the bulbs are mushy where rot sets in as a result of the damage from the feeding millipedes. The immature millipedes are white with two thin reddish-brown rows of dots (spiracles) running down the bottom. These critters are usually detritivorous - in other words they usually only eat dead plants and dead plant parts. It seems they will also eat living plant tissue and will even tunnel into lily (and daffodil) bulbs when their numbers become explosive. This may also be a problem on pot roses and certain houseplants such as poinsettias. There is a chance the nema-tode biological control (Biosafe) will work on this problem. Reducing the amount of peat moss added to the soil is a better long-term solution.

• Botrytis (not pictured here) is a fungal disease which can spread quickly in cool damp weather. At the first sign of brown dots on lily leaves, remove the affected leaves and throw them out. As the disease advances, the brown dots join in larger brown patches, and finally the leaves turn completely brown, collapse and hang limply from the stem. Don't think about it too long before you act, or botrytis may spread to the other lilies in your collection.

There are some baseball-size blobs on my rose stems and when I cut one open it had white, worm-like things in it.

This time of year, the rose stem girdler becomes obvious because the feeding of the beetle larvae (*Agrilus aurichalceus*) distorts and swells the rose stems. These seem to become a problem in one neighbourhood at a time and gradually fan out. In August, the "grubs" are still feeding, so the most effective control is to clip off the swollen growth just below the gall and garbage the galls immediately. This is not really a good time to prune roses, so next summer, look for these swellings earlier in the summer and prune them out as soon as you see them. Constant cutting out of affected growth should eliminate this problem over time. If you do not remove the galls, the beetle grubs will keep feeding until October and then will overwinter in the gall. Look again for further damage this winter because the stems of the rose will be easier to see once the leaves have dropped. 🍃

"My favourite pink lily in the garden is 'Montreaux'. It has the strength and sturdiness of a yellow or orange lily. It is good for cutting and using in bold summer floral arrangements; I just love it."
Patty Bretin, Bretin's Flower Farm

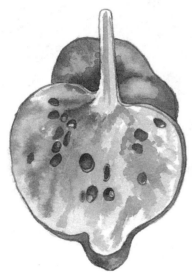

Cut these swellings out as early as possible to prevent the spread of rose stem girdler.

161

Chapter Nine
S·E·P·T·E·M·B·E·R

Winding Down

*W*ill it freeze or won't it? We split our time between worrying about frost, trying to prevent damage from it, and giving up. The flowers sturdy enough to give us colour through a touch of frost are suddenly our favourites. The shrubs and trees are starting to give us spectacular yellows, oranges, and glorious reds, especially from mountain ash, linden, birch, dogwood, nannyberry, cranberry, and Amur maple. Fall-blooming perennials provide a little last minute nectar for the fall-emerging butterflies, especially those butterflies preparing to migrate south.

A few perennials - Siberian iris and peonies - are best divided in the fall. Tender perennials and bulbs are rescued while vegetable harvests continue. It is the morning chill followed by the afternoon warmth that is misleading. Should we just give it up and pull all the tomato plants, or give it another week and hopefully harvest a few more vine-ripened ones? There isn't a clear call or way to predict weather and only one thing is for sure - fall is on the way and we had best prepare for it. There is no point forcing growth in trees, shrubs, and perennials. We need to let them wind down for fall and encourage them to begin the hardening stage. We shouldn't tamper with plant behaviour by increasing fertilizers or watering at this time.

The compost pile is getting so full it is threatening to demand its own city lot, but that's fine. The whole pile will be working quickly over the next few weeks of long days and warm afternoons. We may have more finished compost for topping up those perennial beds than we ever thought possible. 🍃

How do you keep squirrels out of the garden?

I know that special rodent repellents, elemental sulphur, and trip wires don't work. Immediately after working in the garden, sprinkle a layer of peat moss on the soil surface and then wet it down. This works best in the fall, immediately after planting bulbs, especially if it snows or freezes shortly afterwards. The

Black squirrel (Sciurus carolinensis) with a tulip bulb (left).

To Do This Month:
🍃 *Divide Siberian iris and peonies if they need it.*

🍃 *Monitor and moderate watering and slow down on the lawn mowing.*

🍃 *Cover the tender plants at night or wash the frost off early in the morning.*

🍃 *Collect seeds from perennials and promising veggies.*

squirrels can't smell the bulbs or the human scent once the peat moss is laid down and wet. A mixture of bloodmeal and elemental sulphur may have the same disorientating effect on the squirrel's sense of smell.

Unfortunately, unless you also blindfold the squirrels, they may watch your activity and investigate purely out of curiosity right after you have completed the task of planting bulbs or seeds. This is why there is only one sure way to keep the squirrels from digging. Lay chicken wire over the flower beds, and cut out openings to go over and around the plants. This is such a clumsy and difficult procedure that most people limit their efforts to areas of newly planted bulbs, and just hope for the best in the rest of the garden.

To keep squirrels out of bird feeders, the American Backyard Bird Society has developed an all-natural product called "Squirrel Away". It contains capsicum, which is basically ground up chili peppers. The squirrels hate the flavour and ABBS claims it creates a "mental" barrier for squirrels without harming birds. I use it myself because I love bird-watching and I hate how squirrels destroy feeders and scare away birds. It works!

Could you please provide some information concerning mushroom rings in lawns? How can I get rid of them? Is there anything to put on the rings to eliminate them? I've heard several "old wive's tales" on how to do away with fairy ring but haven't tried these cure-alls. In past years, I left the clippings on the lawn because I didn't have a grass catcher. My new mower has a catcher so it all goes into the compost now.

I have mushrooms all over my lawn. What can I do?

From a follow up call to you, I am convinced you are taking excellent care of your lawn: leaving it quite long, cutting weekly, watering, and fertilizing. Continue to power rake in the spring,

164

but add aerating to your spring work as well. This helps to move moisture and nutrients past the thatch and into the rooting zone of the lawn. When the soil is moist in the spring, the power aerator removes nice long plugs of soil.

In late May, when you add the first spring fertilizer to the lawn, don't attempt to control weeds with your fertilizer unless there is a weed problem. Your preventative efforts may be unnecessary. Adding a maximum of 500 grams of actual nitrogen per 100 square metres of lawn each time you fertilize is plenty. Calculate the amount you need by translating the quantity listed on the bag into "actual" quantities of nitrogen. A ten kilogram bag of fertilizer with a 10-10-10 ratio listed on the bag contains 10% nitrogen, or one kilogram of actual nitrogen which is enough for 200 square metres. If the nitrogen is in a slow release formula, more may be added at one time because it will become available over a long period. For easy reference, most bags of fertilizer now specify "covers 200 metres" or "covers 500 metres" or whatever the quantity in the bag will cover. Remember, if you still measure and look at your lawn in square feet, 100 square metres is approximately the same as 1,000 square feet which is the average size of a front yard. The amount of nitrogen fertilizer added is crucial. In effect, the green, vigorous lawn will mask the fairy ring which, as you implied, is impossible to eliminate.

Unfortunately, fairy ring is a naturally-occurring prairie fungus which is always in the air; once it is in your ground it may go as deep as three metres making it hard to remove. Although there are several ring-causing fungus, the most common type here is *Marasmius oreades*. Your excellent lawn care, good quantities of nitrogen, and follow up hand-aerating throughout the summer will make the ring almost disappear. Aerate as often as time allows. Hand aerators look like garden forks but aren't forks. They have hollow tines which, like the power aerators, remove plugs of soil from the lawn. Garden forks and

...The quantity of some kinds of air pollutants produced by running a gasoline-fuelled lawn mower for one hour is about equal to the quantity emitted by a typical automobile driven for 50 miles.[50]

the relatively new "aerator shoes" may do more harm than good because rather than relieving compaction by removing cores of soil, they increase it by pushing down into already compacted soil.

Once the fairy ring is opened up by the removal of soil plugs, it will allow more moisture penetration. Soap mixed with water sometimes allows the waxy, water-resistant coating on the fungus to absorb water and, in the end, the dry, dead patch greens up again. There is also some feeling the fairy rings themselves will stop other fairy rings from growing, so people have inserted pieces of one ring into other rings. It's worth a try.

Most of the miracle and secret cures available on the market are combinations of products to decrease the dryness of the ring (i.e., soap), and mask the damage (i.e., dilute fertilizer) while encouraging a healthy lawn.

So, focus on hiding the damage rather than eliminating a naturally-occurring airborne and invisible enemy. Pick any fairy ring mushrooms you see during the summer and either toss them out or cook them up. They are edible, and apparently have an anchovy-paste flavour when mixed with oil! Of course, you have to make sure it is fairy ring fungus you are picking and not some other toxic look-alike. Check a field guide to see the differences.

It is September and my mums (chrysanthemums) didn't flower. Can you tell me why?

These plants are so frustrating in cool climates; it is a shame. Only the types which mature quickly will produce good fall blooms. All others will be slow to set flower buds, and then will get caught in an early fall frost. Although they can tolerate some cool fall weather, hard frosts will kill the emerging flowers. Try some of the prairie-bred mums like those in the 'Morden' series - 'Morden Garnet' and 'Morden Gold'. They

50. From the Brooklyn Botanic Garden Plants & Garden News Vol 8, No 4, 1993.

start blooming by late July and won't be a disappointment.

Many people have started looking more at the fall blooming asters as a replacement for mums. Try the shortest types you can find, especially the *Aster dumosa* and *Aster amellus* cultivars which are more disease resistant than the *Aster novi-belgii* types. Good garden centres will be able to help you select the ones best for your yard.

When a bromeliad flower dies and comes loose from the main plant, what do you do with the plant (if anything)? Also, if a baby bromeliad comes up alongside the main plant do you remove and replant it?

Tug gently at the dead flowers to remove them. They will pull free if you give them a little twist and tug. You could also just cut out the fading flowers before they fade too far. Small offsets, or "babies", can be left intact because they will grow up to replace the aging plants.

Where can we get the magenta and green varieties of burning bush we have seen in gardens this fall? Also, what care do they need and are they shade or sun loving plants?

There are two plants commonly known as burning bush. One is the annual plant *Kochia scoparia trichophylla* - a less favourable common name is Russian thistle. The name "burning bush" is a tribute to their great fall colour. They are annuals, which means they are started from seed directly outdoors, or they are planted in the spring as bedding plants. They will not survive the winter; they grow quickly, set seed, and die. They are in the genus *Kochia* which makes them closely related to our well known tumbleweed, a plant occasionally used as a Christmas tree by early settlers. Burning bush may even be crossing over the line and becoming weeds in some places due to their vigour.

When the fall conditions are right, burning bush will suddenly turn bright crimson purple as you have described. This gives us an extra month or more of colour in the garden before they die.

There is a lot of variation in both the size and colour of plants; many don't change colour at all in the fall, and others are intensely red. The new cultivar 'Evergreen' is reported to stay uniformly green all season and into the fall. Generally, *Kochia* prefers dry soil and bright sun, but will do great in almost any good garden soil. Once established, they will often reseed, so be careful not to weed out the young seedlings next spring. Many greenhouse growers now report *Kochia* does not grow well in the greenhouse. It seems to go to seed very early, which may be due to a shortage in micronutrients. Plants sprout and then go to seed when they are only a few inches high which has discouraged many growers from offering these as bedding plants. If you can't find them at your garden centre next spring, try direct seeding them directly outdoors if you want *Kochia*.

The other plants with the common name "burning bush" are shrubs: *Euonymus alata* (dwarf burning bush) and *Euonymus turkestanica nana* (Turkestan burning bush). This confusion between common names is the reason many gardeners eventually give in and learn the Latin names for the plants they grow. The shrub burning bush is brilliant red in the fall if the conditions are right. The Turkestan burning bush also has interesting hot pink flowers.

I have seen greenhouse flowers with clusters of multi-coloured blooms from pink to pinkish-orange to yellow all in the same flower. Do you know what they are? Will they grow outdoors in a cold climate?

You must be thinking of *Lantana*! It is a perennial in milder climates but you could try growing it as an annual here. It is easy to start from cuttings, and has very unusual flowers. They start out as yellow, and gradually fade to orange and then pink. This is a trick the flower uses to attract butterflies. The insects are attracted by the huge flower size which is really just a cluster of many smaller flowers. As the pollen sheds and is no longer available to the butterflies, the flowers change from their original yellow colour. The butterflies learn to read the changes in the flower colour, and gradually only go to the newest flowers which are yellow. This changing of colours is a neat trick over 76 different types of plants use to advise their pollinators when lunch is ready and when the restaurant is closed. Take a closer look at forget-me-nots next spring. The centre of the petal is yellow initially and gradually fades to white - another insect cue.

What is the advised care of clematis concerning fertilizer? I was unable to get blooms this year.

Avoid accidentally fertilizing with nitrogen on lawn areas adjacent to clematis. Add bone meal or fertilizers containing phosphorus when you do fertilize. New specialty "clematis fertilizers" have all three main ingredients- nitrogen, phosphorus and potassium- in very low numbers. You could try these or any dilute solution of a complete fertilizer. If you have had trouble with blooms chances are you have a type of clematis which blooms only on old wood. These hardy, old-fashioned plants may lose a season of bloom after a particularly hard winter. Many people prefer the summer blooming kinds of clematis which bloom on the current season's new twigs so the plant doesn't need to overwinter flower buds. There are also clematis which bloom on both old and new wood. These types hedge your bet because if the winter buds are lost, new ones form in the summer.

Some really excellent kinds of clematis include: *Clematis Viticella venosa violaceae*, *C.* 'Etoile Violette', *C.* 'Ernest Markham', *C.* 'Prairie Traveller's Joy', *C.* 'Hagley Hybrid'', *C.* 'Blue Bird', *C.* 'Markham's Pink', and *C. alpina* 'Ruby'. To ensure you only buy the types which bloom on new wood when

Is bone meal a bonus? "Bone meal fertilizer used to have formulas of 10% or 12% nitrogen, and 20% to 25% phosphorus. Today's products have 0-5% nitrogen and 5-10% phosphorus. Every good gardener used to have a bone grinder and they used fresh ground raw bone but today's product is useful largely because it has no effect and it gives the gardener something he thinks is doing good."[51]

51. Avant Gardener, Page 51, Vol 25, N0 7. May 1993.

you first get started with clematis, buy the ones with information of the tags which indicates "late blooming" or "summer blooming" or "pruning type C". These three statements usually mean the plant will bloom on new spring growth, so you won't miss the bloom due to winterkill of flower buds.

What can I do with a butterfly pupa brought indoors?

Put it back where you found it. Pinning it to cedar siding through the silk at the very end of the pupa is one way to re-attach it to something outdoors. Most pupae forming at this time of year are adapted to overwintering that way, and should not be brought in. They need the cool temperatures to trigger spring emergence.

When is it safe to collect willow for wreaths and willow baskets and how do you store it once it is collected?

Collect from November to February or until the buds begin to swell in late winter. Once the buds are swelling, the willow is preparing for spring and the sap is moving. Any cutting at that time could set the plant back and weaken it. Once harvested, bundle and store in a cool place such as the north side of your house out of the direct sun or wind. If the climate is unseasonably mild, or if you must collect it months before using it, store willow in a garbage bag in your freezer until you need it.

Grow willow in your own garden for the easiest access to basket making materials. Cuttings taken in winter may be stored in a plastic bag in the fridge until spring. It is also possible to take small cuttings in spring, start them in water in a brown-glass jar (light encourages algae and discourages rooting) and then stick them in the garden. They will grow rapidly even in the first year.

What is the best way to get rid of a poplar tree?

Wait until spring and remove it when it is at its lowest energy cycle, just as it is reaching full leaf. (See also May.)

There was a beautiful, pink blooming flower in several gardens this summer which looked like a short and single-flowering hollyhock. What was it?

It is silvercup lavatera and it is in the same family as hollyhocks. It is available from several seed catalogues, garden centres, and even on seed stands in grocery stores in the spring. It is easy to start in the home and should be moved outdoors when quite small, so don't start it before early April. Alternately, you may want to direct seed it in the garden in mid-April. Allow seeds to form and turn black in the fall before twisting the ripe seed pod to free the seeds and allow them to scatter. It is great to see lavatera regrow in the spring from seed shaken from the old plants the previous fall. These "free" seedlings make lavatera a very cheap long-term annual flower for almost any garden and they look great with sunflowers which also reseed themselves and grow about the same height as the lavatera.

Lavatera is another 'no sweat' plant for your garden.

Is it necessary to mulch old beds of perennials with leaves in the fall?

No, established flower beds don't usually need mulching; but yes if there are any new divisions or plantings in the bed, or if the bed was reworked this summer and peat moss was added.

In some extreme cases, where the new plant is watered in carefully without mulch or without much attention given to the surrounding soil, the little four inch pot plugs of peat surrounding the new plants become frozen solid in a block of ice. They will pop up above the surrounding soil which may not be as moist or may freeze at a different rate due to the differences in the soil (i.e., less peat). This is called heaving, or frost heaving. It has some complicated relation to physics because the different soil materials expand and contract at different rates when frozen. Peat moss, and the water it holds, tends to freeze and thaw at a different rate than other soil components and when beds have been reworked to add peat moss, I have seen fairly large perennials heaved out of the soil over the winter.

New plants are usually in peaty soil when purchased from the nursery. These new plants may be heaved out of the surrounding soil if they are not mulched. The mulching doesn't stop the differential freezing, but rather it keeps the soil beneath it more evenly moist. The plant is only damaged when it pops out of the soil, usually in the spring, because the exposed roots dry out. If plants do pop out of the soil, don't push them back in - this might damage the roots further. If the soil is thawed, carefully dig up the plant and re-position back in place. If the soil is frozen, mound a little extra soil or mulch around the popped-out plant to keep the roots from being exposed.

Where flower beds are mulched with leaves, the leaves tend to blow around for a week or two until the natural decomposing fungi start to glue the leaf mass together. Laying chicken wire from your pea patch over the leaf-mulched plants in the fall prevents this blowing around. In the spring, especially on the shady side of the house, these leaves may be tough to rake off. Other alternatives to leaf mulch in the fall are: home-made compost or mushroom factory compost about an inch thick on all soil surfaces, woodchips, or cut up Christmas trees which may be placed over the snow or exposed soil in January. If your choice of mulch is leaves, run your lawn mower over the leaves first so they are partially shredded before use.

What can we do about deer? They are eating everything in our garden.

Ingenious homeowners bothered by deer who ravenously munch almost every plant, including mugo pines and cedars (but not Junipers), have observed that a heavy cord tied above a rear fence at deer-eye level seems to discourage the deer from jumping the fence and entering the yard. This only works in settings where fencing is a possibility. Acreages or farm sites aren't as likely to be fenced and the owners will have to resort to other tactics to discourage deer.

Five more deer deterrents:

1. Fabric softener sheets hung around the garden and replaced after several rains work very well.

2. A motion detector that sets off floodlights and an intermittent sprinkler that stays on until deer leave.[52]

3. Milorganite, a soil conditioner and fertilizer will repel deer when applied once or twice a month during the growing season.[53]

4. Set up a miniature, mobile electric fence with thin fibreglass poles and an electric fence kit from a hardware or home supply store. Move this fence around as needed, because the thin rods are easily pushed into the ground and the wires moved up and down depending on the size of predator, gopher or deer![54]

5. A **minimum eight foot high fence** is needed to keep deer away from your trees and plants.

__Rheum palmatum__ is a hardy, unusual perennial for big gardens.

52. The Avant Gardener, Pg 32, Vol. 25, No. 4, February 1993.

53. Milorganite Fertilizer as a Deer Repellent, American Nurseryman 175(6):105 March 15, 1992.

54. Personal discussions with Roger Swain, editor of Horticulture magazine and host of the Victory Garden. March 1995.

Chapter Ten
O·C·T·O·B·E·R

How Not to "Put the Garden to Bed"

$\mathcal{T}$he gardening season is winding down but all kinds of questions have been left unanswered. Is there any way to recoup the season's failures by pouring your heart out now? Will "fall clean-up" and "putting your garden to bed" in October erase all the summer's mistakes?

No. Fall gardening shouldn't be high energy. Many tasks are possible, few are essential. Still, gardeners feel if they can discover what went wrong over the summer or begin their planning while the season is fresh in their minds, they will get a head start on next spring. I usually counsel relaxation... "putting a garden to bed" isn't necessary. The gradual reduction in water, the absence of fertilizer, and the increasingly cooler nights do most of the work for you.

If you insist, there are a few tasks to do this month.

The garden soil has been rock hard all summer. Is there anything which can be done in the fall to improve it?

It is an excellent time of year to upgrade the soil. This might mean spreading your own compost over the garden soil. Alternately, purchase and topdress with peat, manure, or spent mushroom compost. While home-made compost is free, peat moss is often expensive in the fall, and mushroom manure might be tough to get if you don't have a truck or live near a mushroom factory. It is always preferable to lay "organics" in a layer on top of the soil, rather than working them into the soil.

Farmyard manure has the disadvantage of coming complete with weed seeds although mushroom compost has been heat sterilized so it won't include weeds. Either way, add no more than two centimetres of manure or mushroom compost on top of the soil because both forms have a variable but plentiful source of nitrogen which may cause a late spurt of growth in plants.

Another quick way to start working towards better soil is to avoid fall rototilling. The organic component of our soils has

Autumn leaves (left).

To Do This Month:
🍂 *Improve soil.*
🍂 *Cut back perennials.*
🍂 *Transplant evergreens.*
🍂 *Mulch perennial and shrub beds.*
🍂 *Take cuttings from geraniums.*
🍂 *Make sure to give your trees and shrubs a really good soak after they drop their leaves.*

dropped drastically since the dawn of fall tilling. Current thought dictates working the soil as little as possible. This allows the weed seeds to stay buried and the roots of the dying garden plants to stay intact where they will decompose. Soil turned over and exposed to the air quickly loses organic matter.

Some cities and municipalities such as Edmonton pick a day in the fall to give away the municipal compost and only ask that you bring your own container. Phone the recycling council or Parks department in your closest town or city for details.

If you aren't overworking your soil and have plenty of organic matter, the only other problem might be your clay content is high and this is leading to the hardness. Products like "Clay Buster" will break up hard worm castings and clumpiness in soils with too high a clay level. Give it a try.

"...the higher the organic matter in the soil, the higher its ability to support beneficial microbes which suppress soil-borne disease."[55]

I have recently planted a green ash tree and have heard it should be pruned as soon as it is planted. Some of the branches are broken and the tree has lost all its leaves. Should I prune it?

No! Emphatically no. Do not believe the old practice of pruning following planting "just to even things out". The old theory went this way: If you move a tree, you disturb the roots and that means there will be fewer roots than top growth, so remove up to one-third of the top-growth to compensate. This is now frowned upon. First, how do you know you have damaged 30% of the roots? Many trees are now sold in containers, and you will not damage or remove the roots at all. Second, while it is true the tree will be set back by the trans-planting process, why not let the tree tell you how far it has

55. The Avant Gardener, Pg 1, Vol. 25, No. 5. March 1993.

been set back, and which branches are affected? Removing branches now will remove terminal buds which are needed to promote root development.

Also, roots are connected to specific branches, but the branches directly above the roots aren't necessarily the ones connected by the "veins" of the tree. The tree's vascular system spirals and twists around the trunk, a fact which can be verified by looking at an old dead tree.

In other words, instead of trying to determine which branches may have been affected by the shock of transplant, let the tree tell you. It will do this by allowing unproductive branches to die. Any that don't leaf out next spring are dead. Remove them in June.

The broken branches are more of a problem. They shouldn't be allowed to dangle from the tree all winter; broken branches should be removed promptly regardless of the season. (See February for correct pruning cuts.)

My pussy willow tree (*Salix discolor*) has aphids every summer. If I spray it will this hurt the pussy-willows in the spring?

This dead limber pine shows why it can be difficult to decide what branches might be connected by the same roots.

If your pussy willow tree has aphids, try using dormant oil next spring.

There is always a tree or shrub in every neighbourhood that attracts aphids and becomes the "roosting" tree come fall. If your willow has become infested this way, try spraying it with dormant oil in the spring. Dormant oil is just a very fine mineral oil, so it won't hurt the environment but it will suffocate the overwintering aphids. Make sure to spray just before the leaves come out next spring and wear a face mask yourself. Very fine oil could harm human lungs, so be careful. Pussy willows are the male flower buds and they will not be harmed by dormant oil because they will be fully expanded and flowering by the time the dormant oil is applied.

I planted a twelve foot tall (four metre) Austrian pine in June and it has started to turn brown on the inside. Is the tree going to die?

No. It is pretty typical of evergreens, especially pines, to cut their losses in the fall and shed a few leaves. Although they are evergreen, pine needles as individuals only live five to seven years. In the fall, the tree does a cost analysis on leaf worth and sheds the ones that are low producers. These include leaves shaded within the tree, or very old leaves. If the tree is under any kind of stress, such as the newly transplanted Austrian pine (*Pinus nigra*) in your yard, it will likely shed more than the normal amount of needles. You don't have to start really worrying about the tree dying unless the new needles turn brown next spring.

I put in some strawberry divisions in the spring and the plants got dry, and then it rained so much and they got water-logged. Now they have begun to send out long runners and to flower. Should I remove these flowers and runners? I have heard you should do this in the first year. Also, when should I mulch them for the winter?

The logic behind removing the flowers goes like this: a plant expends more energy producing flowers and fruit than leaves, so in the first year many people remove the flowers to reduce this energy loss and to encourage building up energy in the crown of the plant. I have been told by a commercial strawberry grower that it made no difference to his crop when he pinched half the flowers on his crop and left the other half untouched on newly transplanted strawberries.[56]

This result may vary with different types of strawberries, and in your case, with the blooms coming so late I would say go ahead and remove the flowers, but not the new growth. Also, stop watering and do not fertilize at this time.

Wait to mulch your strawberries until after the soil has frozen, so you are not insulating the soil against frost and providing a haven for the mice. Depending on the fall, this may mean mulching after it snows.

There are cones on the top 30 centimetres of my spruce tree in Edmonton. This looks ugly; I would like to know if it will hurt the tree to remove this top section?

It won't **hurt** the tree excessively, but it will ruin the look of the tree. You will be left without a leader, and by next spring, two or three of the top branches will attempt to take over as leader and this will cause more work for you and will further disfigure the tree. I would recommend removing the cones by hand picking, rather than removing the top of the tree.

I started some lavender plants this spring and I have over wintered lavender outdoors before in Edmonton, but I was wondering if I could bring it indoors. Or does it require a cold period to continue growing?

Lavender may be brought in but will need the best light possible once in the house. Like you, I have overwintered lavender outside but never inside. I have brought rosemary indoors in the winter, though, and the two plants are very

---

56. Discussions with Al Schernus, The Garden, 1993.

similar in look and overall requirements. I believe it will work for you.

If you decide to bring lavender in for the winter, make sure to wash the plant carefully to avoid bringing aphids in with it. I recommend wrapping a plastic bag over the pot and soil, then turning the whole plant upside down and swishing it around in a sink or deep bucket of warm sudsy water. This swishing action and soap combination will dislodge any aphids trying to get in out of the cold. Bringing in pests with your outdoor plants is the only risk I foresee with your lavender. The new All America Selection of lavender is called "Lavender Lady". It is a very quick growing variety which blooms the first year from seed and overwinters outdoors without protection.

My birch tree was greatly damaged five years ago in a wind storm. I pruned it back then, but it hasn't regained its nice shape. Will it ever look good again? It is over twenty years old.

A mature birch tree absolutely hates to be pruned. Because of the major damage that occurred I can understand why you pruned it but I can also understand why the tree has not regrown. Depending on the time of year when the tree was damaged and pruned, it could have suffered badly to terribly badly from the wind and the pruning. Because it still hasn't come back, I suggest the damage was irreparable, and the new growth, if any, will be weak and easily damaged. It sounds like this tree is toast! Buy a new one. (For tree removal strategies see May.)

I have heard you can collect seeds from your garden but you shouldn't put them in film canisters because there isn't enough air. What do you think?

Actually, film canisters work great. Make sure to allow the seed to dry completely in a loose paper bag before you separate the seed from the chaff and store it in the film containers. If the seed is not completely dry, it will mildew in any airtight container, so make sure it is dry. Separating the seed from the chaff takes some practice and either some small screens or a piece of paper. Shift the seed back and forth on the paper or through the screens to clean it. Once clean, put the seed in the fridge or freezer. Cold storage ensures slower respiration which means the seed will last longer and be in better condition over the long haul.

Some people prefer to use baby food jars or old coffee cans with plastic lids. In the case of coffee cans, keep the seed in small envelopes within the can. Some seed is just so tiny it gets lost or stuck in the cracks of an ordinary envelope. Envelopes used by stamp collectors are ideal because they are very small and self-sticking. Purchase these special envelopes at stamp collecting shops.

My honeysuckle has witch's broom, and I have tried spraying it with malathion and removing the witches' brooms in the summer, but more damage keeps appearing. What should I do?

Unfortunately, the aphid which causes witch's broom has become a real problem on Tatarian honeysuckles (*Lonicera tatarica*). These are the older, larger, coarser honeysuckle shrubs of farm yards and older neighbourhoods. Other types of honeysuckle are not as susceptible. It doesn't surprise me that the malathion you tried didn't work. It isn't registered for this use and it doesn't work in the right way to reach these aphids which are protected within the distorted and frenzied leaves of the affected honeysuckle. Pruning off the new growth as it shows the symptoms is good, but as you have found out it takes diligence and ongoing action. The trimmed and damaged branches cannot be composted but must be thrown away or burned. The cutting must be repeated often. Many people find this is too much work and they simply choose to remove the

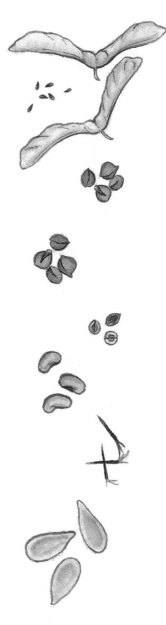

Collecting your own seeds can be very rewarding.

shrub. It is not an easy decision.

Cats are highly attracted to any type of honeysuckle, so if you are growing yours as an attraction for your cats, try instead the dwarf, aphid-resistant forms of honeysuckle.

We have some weird death symptoms on our spruce trees which are now 20 feet tall and several years old. Entire and seemingly unrelated branches are turning red. The needles just turn this rusty brown colour and then they fall off. What is wrong?

The damage you describe sounds like the tree is suffering from cytospera canker. If it was simply the expected fall shedding of needles, only the innermost needles along the main trunk or inner branches would be affected. Look for oozing of a golden liquid near the base of the affected branches; you may have to wait now until next spring to see this. Unfortunately there isn't really a cure for this disease and improving tree health which means reducing stress to the tree is the only option. Very young trees may die from these cankers, but older trees usually only lose a few branches and then the situation corrects itself when the cultural controls are improved.

I am thinking of resodding a portion of my backyard, but we have a lot of weeds in the existing lawn. We want to treat it first with Round-Up™. Will this work?

I recommend calling the chemical manufacturers or reading the label on the product in absolutely every case when I am questioned about the use of a chemical. Please do this before using the herbicide Round-Up which was developed originally and manufactured by the Monsanto Company. Residential, ready to use formulations are now available under several different trade names. In your particular application, I would hold off using a grass-killing spray of this type at this time. It is late in the fall, the grass hasn't even been cut for a few weeks, and the weeds and grasses certainly won't be growing or actively absorbing herbicides either. You may end up wasting the product and not getting the results you want. You might be successful hand-digging some of the weeds and exposing their roots over winter. Get right back on it in the spring and, following some general soil improvement measures, lay that new sod. Alternately, improve your lawn care procedures, keep the old lawn, and save yourself a lot of work. (See April for basic lawn care.)

We have a mature shelterbelt and were told to mulch it with at least six inches of straw to help it grow. Straw carries a lot of seed including weed seed, so we are worried there will be a real weed problem there next spring. Also, won't this just attract mice?

Yes, on both counts. Mulch is good for trees but straw mulch will **certainly** spread weeds and attract mice. Old leaves or woodchips (made from old prunings or delivered from your utility company) are preferable as mulches instead of straw. Even shredded newspaper is a preferable mulch to straw with some plants.[57]

Regardless of the mulch used, the rule of thumb is to use **no more** than four inches of mulch which means four inches (ten centimetres) is the maximum amount of mulch to use, not the minimum. A wood chip mulch encourages the soil microbes which repay the tree by dying and in turn supplying nutrients to the tree. Other microbes working actively with the tree roots are the mycorrhizae; they allow for more efficient intake of nutrients. Trees with a healthy mycorrhizae population are healthier.

Utility companies and local landscapers handle large quantities

If straw is the only mulch you have, try solarizing it before using it. Do this by spreading it on the soil or on pavement. Moisten and cover with black plastic for two to three weeks.

57. "Shredded Newspaper vrs. Wheat Straw as Mulches", Abstract 5199, Horticultural Abstracts 63(7), July 1993, 658. (C.A.B. International, Wallingford, Oxford, 0X10 8DE, United Kingdom). "... Yields were highest for all crops with newspaper mulch. Adding large amounts of shredded newspaper to the soil did not result in accumulation of potentially hazardous heavy metals." Tests were conducted on sweet corn, soybeans, and tomatoes.

of waste from their pruning operations and they usually chip their waste to minimise dumping charges at the landfill sites. They are often willing to give chips away to clients or to sell them for a small handling fee.

"Organic mulches **without** underlying plastic materials reduced total weeds by 50%, although there were no significant differences among different mulches... while polyethylene prevents the establishment of perennial weed species, its lack of porosity has been associated with reduced plant growth..."[58]

There is a mountain ash tree in our yard which is seven feet tall and still has green leaves. Can I move it right now?

No. A tree with green leaves in October is obviously in trouble. Perhaps because it is in a protected location and hasn't had the full effect of the frost yet, perhaps it isn't hardy, or possibly, it has been watered and fertilized too late in the growing season. Either way, it is best to encourage this tree to change colour by holding back water. Approximately four to six weeks after the leaves are shed, the root hairs will have shed, and it will be safe to move the tree. Unfortunately, because this tree is so late in changing, it may be too late to move it this fall. Keep your eyes on it, and if the fall stays mild and the soil is not frozen by the time it is safe to move the tree, then move it, water it, and mulch it. Fall moving is desirable for evergreens but most other trees are best moved in the spring.

We have a Mayday tree in our back yard and it has sprouted on the alley side of the fence and developed almost an entirely new tree on that side. The tree is just starting to colour up for fall. Can we safely remove this large branch now?

58. W.A. Skroch (Dept. of Horticultural Science, North Carolina State University, Raleigh, NC, 27695), M.A. Powell, T.E. Bilderback, and P.H. Henry, "Mulches: Durability, Aesthetic Value, Weed Control, and Temperature", Journal of Environmental Horticulture 10(1), March 1992, 43-45.

No. The best time to remove new suckers is in early to mid-August during the first year they sprout. This way they have had a chance to give something back to the tree before they are removed. I don't like to encourage pruning while a tree is going through its fall transition, because this will force the tree to react to the wound rather than prepare for winter. Your tree sucker is so large I would leave it now until a few weeks after it has reached full leaf next June. Because this is such a mature sucker, indeed almost tree size, if you remove it in the winter the energy stored in the tree's roots will greatly exceed the top growth and the tree will respond by sending out even **more suckers** in the spring.

Many Mayday trees sucker because they are planted too deep initially. Refer to the drawing of correct tree planting (in May) to review the current thought on this subject.

My neighbour has native roses he wants to give me but I'm not sure when to move them. They are still green.

Native roses are pretty tough. They can be moved late into the fall, well after they have lost their leaves, without danger. Some people get tired of doing heavy garden work in the fall and prefer to prepare the site in the fall, but delay the transplanting until spring. It really doesn't matter in the case of native roses. As long as you wait until well after the leaves have dropped this fall before attempting the move you will be okay... unless there is snow on the ground by that time.

We have no flower beds in our new house but I would like to plant bulbs. Could I do this in planters or pots?

Yes, this is a wonderful idea. Plant them up in pots, and then sink the pots into the ground in your vegetable garden. Mulch the area above the pots with 15 centimetres of leaves or any other loose, light, available mulch. Gradually remove the mulch in the spring after the snow melts, and then dig the pots and move them to your deck or wherever you need colour.

Rubber chopped into 1/4 inch crumbs or smaller was added to the top 15 centimetres of playing field soil at several Michigan sites to reduce compaction in the fields and to dispose of the rubber. "Adding 20% (chopped up) rubber (into the soil) worked well for Kentucky Bluegrass and Ryegrass plots".[59]

Some people plant several layers of bulbs within one large pot to have a succession of bloom. Deeply planted daffodils may also be overplanted in the spring with blue pansies for a beautiful two-tiered look in pots. The bulbs will multiply in the pots and may be sunk in the garden again later in the summer and brought out again year after year.

Another way to bring bulbs through to the spring outside your garden is to plant and water them in pots which are stored in the garage in the fall. The steady cool temperatures in the garage will prevent drying of the soil but should allow the bulbs to get their cool winter spell without too much freezing and thawing. This is still pretty much a hit-and-miss approach which won't be nearly as good as a root cellar or controlled cool room so the timing of bloom won't be as reliable. The pots may have to be further insulated from freezing and thawing if it gets too cold.

There are spruce trees 15 feet high on our farm, but the horses in a near-by pasture have come over recently and eaten the middle out of the trees. Can these trees now be cut back to the ground to regain their nice shape?

This heavy pruning would weaken the trees and they would never regain their shape. In any case they are probably in a bad location if they are within reach of the horses. Consider planting another row further away from the fence in the shelter of what's left of the existing trees, and then plan to completely remove the damaged trees as the new ones take hold. This will be faster in the long run than topping spruce and waiting for it to regrow. If you do want to top them anyway, try leaving a main branch near the ground which can become the new leader. If you remove all the branches the spruce will not sucker up as poplars do; they will just die.

I have heard there are some types of *Lythrum* that shouldn't

59. John Rogers 111, Tim Vanini, and Michael Ventola, "Shredded Tires: A New Soil Amendment", Grounds Maintenance 29(3), March 1994, 42,44,48,49.

be planted in Alberta. Is this true, and how can I tell the different kinds apart?

Lythrum salicaria, also known as loosestrife or lythrum, is a weed that is becoming a problem across Canada and the United States; everyone is now being discouraged from growing any kind of *Lythrum*. Even the hybrid cultivars, which weren't initially considered a problem, should not be grown and are no longer being offered for sale by reputable nurseries including members of the nursery trade associations. If you have *Lythrum* you should remove it regardless of what kind it is. It produces millions of seeds each fall which germinate in moist areas including the very best duck habitats. The ducks suffer because they can't use the *Lythrum* for anything and it competes with the plants the ducks need to eat and to build their nests with. These other plants just can't outcompete *Lythrum*.

If you know of an out-of-control patch on private or public land, there is a *Lythrum* hotline number where it can be reported. Call 1-800-565-6305.

Try growing *Liatris,* Veronica, or perennial phlox where you need to replace the colour and form of perennial *Lythrum* in your yard.

How do you salvage tuberous begonias and dahlias from the garden?

These plants are both very sensitive to frost. It may be too late in the season already to be thinking of salvaging them. If they have been lightly frosted the leaves will immediately turn black. If they are still green and lush, try digging them and storing them in clumps of soil in a warm dry area until the top growth dies back naturally. The soil can then be broken away and brushed off the corms of the begonias and tubers of dahlias. Make sure the soil is not too wet when the initial digging occurs or you will have trouble getting it off the roots later, especially if it has a high clay content. Do not damage the surface of the corms (small, fleshy, bulb-like roots) or tubers or you may damage dormant buds. Begonias and dahlias may be washed and dried in the sun once the dead plant part and soil are removed. They like to be stored in a box in a cool room in peat moss or vermiculite. The perfect storage temperature is between two to five degrees Celsius (the temperature of your fridge crisper should be in this range but the newer fridges are "frost free" so they dehydrate while they store and are not recommended). Leave a small portion of the stem attached to the dahlia tuber because this is the region where the buds will be initiated. To keep the begonia and dahlia roots from drying out completely, lightly moisten the peat moss or vermiculite before placing the dahlias in storage. The peat or vermiculite should not be noticeably dry or wet, just damp.

By late February or early March the buds on the begonia corms will start to sprout. They should be potted immediately once this begins. Dahlias may be delayed until later in April, but will also benefit from being planted in a pot first and then moved outdoors in June when the weather is warm and the risk of frost is long past. Dahlia habitat is a clearing in the high elevation forests of Central and South America where they expect and receive cool evenings and warm humid days. They don't ever get frost, and at worst, they go through a brief dry spell in the winter when the plant may wither. This is why our winter care is so important. We have to imitate a tropical forest in a prairie climate. I have heard of people being successful overwintering these plants just by shovelling the whole clump, soil and all, into a cardboard box and storing the works in a cool room.

When is the right time to pick rose hips? Do they have to have frost first?

Frost might sweeten the rose hips but it isn't essential to have frost prior to using the hips as long as they are soft and red. It is tricky separating the fruit from the seed, and I recommend using rubber gloves because rose seed has irritating hairs which are sometimes used as itching powder!

Use gloves when separating rose hip fruit from the seed.

I have taken red shale out of my garden paths and now wonder if it can be added to the compost or will it add a toxic chemical? It is well worn and very pulverised.

The shale has crumbled to a fine powder and will be fine as a direct addition to the soil or to the compost bin. It will aid drainage where added to the soil, so do not add it to areas which are already very dry. Instead, lay it on top and perhaps scratch it in slightly this fall wherever the soil is poorly drained or overly moist.

How do you start native dogwood from seed?

Direct seed it, berry and all, in the fall. Alternately, smash the fruit gently, soak it in water for a few days, and then sort through the mush and look for the heavier, more viable seeds, which are likely sitting in the bottom of the jar. Place the seeds in a small amount of damp peat moss in a ziplock baggie. After 30-90 days in the fridge, the seed will begin to germinate. Place each seed or seedling in individual pots at this time and then plant them out in the garden in the spring. Obviously the first approach is easier but the number of seedlings, the germination rate, and placement of seedlings is less predictable.

Because I have so many bird visitors in my garden I often find dogwood seedlings growing. I transplant them around to people-pleasing places whenever I find them.

I have been growing Egyptian onions which form large "onions" on the tip of the flowering stalks and this stalk has fallen over. Does this mean you can't eat the onion in the ground?

You have been growing *Allium cepa* which may reach heights of seven feet tall. This species includes many well known onions such as shallots and the multiplier onion which are usually sterile and reproduced mainly by offsets. The Egyptian onion produces bulbils on the flower stalk and is propagated by these bulbils. This does not affect the flavour of the onion itself. When the flowering stem and leaves fall over, the onions are mature and ready to harvest. If they are not ripening and falling over, bend the leaves and stalks over by hand and harvest the onions a week or two later.

The little onions on the end of the leaves give the plant one more way to reproduce, but they don't take away from the underground storage of nutrients and sugars in the onion bulb. Onions have been cultivated for so many centuries that the origins of many kinds have been lost. This extended historical cultivation of onions has led to continuous propagation by off-sets and bulbils with little need for seed. In other words, onions have historically been selected for non-seeding types. Some garlic plants discovered in Italy in the past decade did produce seed which led scientists to believe they may have discovered the origins of this well known member of the onion family.

How do you overwinter 'Martha Washington' geraniums?

These may be handled as house plants. Unlike other geraniums, which tolerate heavy cutting and cool storage, these prefer to be kept alive. They are intensive nitrogen users and also need intense light. This means they will lose some of the more shaded inner leaves when brought indoors. Compensate by giving them a sunny spot plus fluorescent lights within 30 centimetres of the plant leaves. If leaves drop after the end of October, fertilize with dilute nitrogen. Never let the new growth get long and weak. If the plants are growing too scraggly, pinch the newest tips of growth out with your fingers. This will discourage lanky growth and encourage side sprouting.

By January, plan to reshape the plants slightly and start a more regular fertilizer program. High light and a balanced fertilizer will bring these back into bloom by May.

When should geraniums and fuschias be cut back for winter storage? How far should they be cut, and generally

how should they be handled?

This was partially answered above regarding 'Martha Washington' geraniums. Some people cut geraniums back while others take cuttings and discard the original plant, or as with the 'Martha Washington' variety simply leave the plant intact and allow it to continue to grow until January when the plant is reshaped in preparation for spring flower forcing. Finally, some people clean the plant up thoroughly by washing the leaves and stems in soapy water and then cutting back this top growth, and putting the half-denuded plant in a dark cupboard for winter. They only occasionally check on the plants to give them a meagre amount of water until January, when the plant is taken from the cupboard and regrown from the base plant or from lush cuttings forced from the base plant. Check for insects occasionally during the fall storage period and rewash the plants as needed.

If taking cuttings at any time, remember to allow the 15 centimetre long cuttings to dry overnight on the counter before attempting to root them. They will rot if plunged right into moist vermiculite or sand after being cut from the main plant. The drying on the counter allows the cutting to callous over, which is necessary before roots will develop.

Fuschias may also be kept alive but will likely be harbouring insects so they should also be washed carefully and then kept alive under lights all winter in the same way recommended for 'Martha Washington' geraniums.

Top, 'Martha Washington', bottom, regular geraniums. Geraniums can be kept from year to year by cuttings or just reshaping.

Can apple leaves be used in compost? I have been told they, like walnuts, have poisonous leaves.

Apple seeds, branch bark and, to a lesser degree, the leaves contain trace amounts of cyanide. These quantities are so low they don't pose a real danger to grazing animals, so should not pose a problem to soil if used in compost.[60] In this way, apples

60. Discussions with the Poison Control Centre in Calgary, Fall 1992.

are different from walnuts. There is a chemical in walnut leaves which actually inhibits the growth of other plants. It acts like a herbicide and would be dangerous in compost.

Oaks are also a problem in compost because oak leaves carry tannins which cause an allelopathic response in soils, which means they give off a chemical as they decompose which prevents other things from growing. I heard from a fellow recently who had worked 60 centimetres worth of oak leaves into his already really great garden soil. He effectively killed the soil. All his plants are dying in it so I recommended that he work in activated charcoal which is usually recommended to combat soil-borne pesticides. In a sense, oak leaves are like pesticides because of their allelopathic response in the soil; in nature, the decomposing leaves set up a nice little protection zone for the mother oak tree and prevent everything else from growing. Hard way to learn this lesson.

We have just moved into an older home with a wonderful garden and are wondering if it is absolutely necessary to fertilize the trees and lawn for winter?

No. It is an option. An option which is usually based on a soil test. I hate to see people jump into fall fertilizers just because these fertilizers are available. Nitrogen in fertilizers may cause a late spurt of growth on trees not yet fully hardened or they may keep lawns unnecessarily green too long. Green lawns in the fall run the risk of developing the disease known as "snow mould" under the snow during the winter, especially when we get late snows in early spring. This fungus disease is encouraged by nitrogen rich foliage.

If a soil test points out a shortage of potassium, one of the main winteriser components of fall fertilizer, add some straight potassium chloride (0-0-60). Researchers seem to disagree if lack of potassium leads to reduced winter hardiness or not, but at least one turf expert claims potassium does mean sturdier grass (thickened cell walls).[61]

With trees and shrubs, most experts agree poor fertility throughout the growing season is more to blame for lack of hardiness than lack of nutrients in the fall. Half the recommended rate of a complete fertilizer is sometimes recommended in the fall after leaf colour has started changing.[62] Using fertilizers before leaf colour changes in the fall may prevent or discourage normal fall activity (i.e., movement of nutrients into storage). The logic behind the practise of fall fertilizing is that soils are warmer in fall and the roots more active than they are in early spring so they will be able to make use of the fertilizer.

The worst that will happen if you don't fertilize your lawn in the fall is it will not green up as early in the spring. This may help the lawn if we get a late snow fall because, again, it will discourage fungus diseases. Use a complete fertilizer including iron, especially one with potassium (the third number on the bag of fertilizer) in the spring. (See May for more information on lawn and tree fertilizers.)

I have started lodgepole pine seedlings and they are still in small pots. Can they safely be moved to the garden?

Yes, plant them out immediately before the soil freezes and then mulch them to keep the soil from freezing around them for a short while so they may prepare for fall. Coarse peat moss or leaves will make an excellent loose mulch for young tree seedlings. If mice are a problem in your area, make sure to pull the mulch well away from the trunk of the little trees; the mulch should not be touching the bark.

Something has been eating semi-circle notches out of my rose bushes?

61. "Moderation the Key When Combating Turf Diseases", Dennis McKernan, Turf & Recreation Magazine, Pages 14-15, April/May 1994.

62. Fall Fertilization and Winter Hardiness of Woody Landscape Plants, Christopher Kessel, Nursery Specialist. Pgs 20-22, Landscape Trades, 1993.

You have leaf-cutter bees. They are really out of their range because they are more commonly found where alfalfa is grown than in the middle of the city. They are useful to alfalfa growers because they pollinate the alfalfa and increase the seed set. Because they don't do a lot of damage to rose plants and are so useful in their pollination role, it is probably better to ignore them. Their damage is very curious and unique and noticeable!

Is it possible to grow crab-apples from seed?

Yes, but most crab-apples are hybrid cultivars or clones. They will not come true from seed. Also, the trees available from nurseries have often been grafted with a dwarfing characteristic on the main stem and this will not be present in a seedling. If you have an apple or crab-apple that you really like, it is better to trim graft wood from the desired tree in winter and place it on a seedling or small tree in the growing season. Superior grafted apple seedlings are available from mail-order or local nurseries (see Sources).

Although it is late in the season, I am interested in learning how to dry flowers with silica gel. Where do you get silica gel, and can it be used more than once?

Silica gel is available at most craft and hobby stores. It is cheapest in bulk lots from craft wholesalers. It is used to successfully dry almost any flower except those which are very deep red. Dark red roses, for instance, look almost black when dry. Silica gel may be reused again and again. Spread the silica gel in a shallow pan in the oven at 250 degrees Fahrenheit until the moist pink crystals turn blue. Store dried crystals in an airtight container. Instructions for use and reuse also come on the package.

Remember silica dried flowers are very fragile and cannot tolerate humidity, so they shouldn't be kept in the kitchen.

Are there any hints to growing hops as a climbing vine in the garden in High River?

No special care is needed to grow *Humulus lupulus* (hops) in High River or in any northern garden, but I would advise against working the soil near the plants. The roots are easily damaged, and won't tolerate disturbance. This European introduction is naturalised along the riverbanks in Calgary and many areas so it is definitely hardy; it may grow three metres in a summer. It is a fantastic climbing plant with an interesting aroma. (See May for more information on this perennial vine.)

I have been potting up spruce trees from a road allowance on my property with an eye to "decorating" them and giving them away or selling them for Christmas. Do you foresee any problems with selling live Christmas trees? How should they be treated?

By now, the end of October, your trees have gone fully dormant. If they are potted, they won't survive long in pots with the roots exposed to winter extremes in temperature. They will be most likely to survive if they are sunk into the ground or stored in a cool room or unheated garage with plenty of light. Anything that will keep the soil from freezing solid would be fine. Once brought inside for decorating and displaying over Christmas, the trees cannot be brought back outdoors. They will lose their dormancy during the warm "Christmas Break" and will freeze and suffer winter damage when returned to the outdoors. Instead, after Christmas the young trees could be watered and kept alive in a high light, cool setting. An unheated sunroom may be ideal if the temperatures don't drop below freezing.

Once the soil is thawed outdoors in the spring, plant the trees out, or sink the whole pot in the ground, ready for digging again in the fall, and holding over as a permanent holiday plant. 🍂

Chapter Eleven

N·O·V·E·M·B·E·R &
D·E·C·E·M·B·E·R

It's Late but Not Too Late

*U*nless you force bulbs for Christmas or become an avid bird feeder and watcher, there isn't much activity that's visible in the garden at this time of year. The starving deer and bunnies might be gnawing at your tree trunks, but you'll rarely witness the destruction. Tiny voles may be girdling your prize ginkgo tree, but that's not visible either. Geraniums are long gone to storage, it's too early to start seeds, and the catalogues haven't arrived.

Imagine gazing out into a garden piled high with snow on ever greens and on clumps of brilliant red highbush cranberry or mountain ash fruit. The frost on the birch, red bark of dogwoods, and contrasts in tree architecture provided excellent viewing all winter if the garden is designed for winter viewing.

If you aren't busy redesigning your garden to provide a year round colour splash, put your feet up and read. This is truly the goof update season.

I bought some tulip bulbs earlier this fall and haven't had a chance to plant them yet. Is it too late?

Yes, the best you can do, if they aren't too dried out from storage, is to try forcing these bulbs for winter colour. They need to be potted in soil and stored in a cool spot for 12 weeks or more until they start to sprout. Check the soil occasionally and water it to keep it moist. Bring the pots gradually into a warmer spot and encourage the foliage to grow. Keep them out of direct light once the flowers begin to show colour.

We would like to know the best time to trim a cedar.

In time for your Christmas decorating! Actually, you can prune cedars any time the wood is not frozen. Treat cedars the same as junipers and other evergreens when contemplating pruning. They never go through the massive leaf drop and shock that deciduous plants do, so they do not suffer from a little light pruning almost anytime.

Weeping tree architecture (left).

To Do These Months:
Read.
Care for your house plants (a little dusting never hurts).
Cut back perennials if the snow isn't too deep.
Begin pruning (see pruning chart in June).
Cut evergreen branches and berries for your planter boxes or indoor arrangements.
Buy a flowering plant.

How many times do you water a cactus? I was told weekly.

Make sure you have a well drained soil mix for your cacti and other succulents. You don't want a soil with a high peat moss content or the soil will stay too moist. Once your cactus is in the right soil, top the soil surface with a little coarse sand or crushed granite (#1 or #2 size chicken grit is an excellent mulch for the soil surface of cactus). Once a week should be fine for watering your cactus, but plunge your finger into the soil occasionally to make sure it is not drying out too much or staying too moist.

Is there any one fertilizer or method of fertilizing that will get plants to bloom throughout the winter?

Of course it depends on what types of plants you are talking about, but if you are thinking geraniums brought in from out-doors, or even hibiscus, then it might be necessary to fertilize over the winter. I would prefer if the plants were given a two month rest over winter to allow the extra salts (which are part of the fertilizer) a chance to wash away during normal watering. Begin fertilizing again when the light levels increase again in late February or early March.

How do you encourage new growth on Norfolk Island pines? What do you do if the inside leaves turn brown and start falling off?

Norfolk pines need high humidity and high light but cool temperatures. This makes them very difficult in most people's homes. Setting up a humidifier near your tree will help a great deal. Pruning and trimming of Norfolks isn't really practical. Instead, try to make sure they receive continuous moisture and humidity so they will grow in a regular pattern. A well grown Norfolk is a beautiful sight.

My Kaffir lily has mealy bugs. Is there anything to be done about it? I have tried a spray of rubbing alcohol and water but this didn't work.

This plant is botanically known as *Clivia miniata* and is sometimes called just plain clivia. It has showy bright orange flowers every spring, especially when it is potbound. In commercial buildings any plant worth less than $100 is tossed if it has mealybugs. They are just that hard to control and so persistent. The predatory insect, *Cryptolaemus*, is useful in eating mealybugs, but will not eat them all. Rubbing alcohol only really works if it is placed on the end of a cotton swab and touched individually to each and every mealy bug. This is very labour intensive. An occasional wash with insecticidal soap (available at your garden centres) slows these pests down a bit.

*To start a **clivia** plant from seed, collect the ripe red fruit from a friend's plant in early to midsummer. If you are on holidays in a warm climate you may find clivia growing in the landscapes of hotels and parks. The bright red seed pods are poked whole into the soil with a finger and kept moist for a few weeks until they germinate. They will bloom in three to four years, and should be allowed to get crowded in their pots before transplanting.*

I have a banana tree which I fertilize regularly but the outside edge of the leaves are turning brown. Is there any way to prevent this?

Stop fertilizing, leach the soil, and increase the humidity. These plants are very susceptible to a build up of salts in the soil due to regular fertilizing. In the winter, when the plants aren't using as many nutrients or water, the salt levels build up and cause the symptoms you have described.

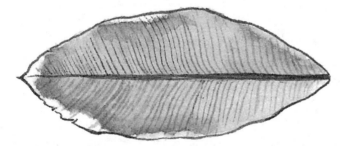

I have just received a Christmas cactus, what are the requirements?

My Christmas cactus is dropping blooms. It is near a south window and is only one week old. Also, how do you bring it back into bloom?

Christmas cactus are best in a north window where they can be

Brown leaf edges can be signs of salt build up.

Christmas cactus

Azalea

left undisturbed for thirty years... well, maybe not that long, but definitely the key to success is to leave the plant in one position once it comes home. Constant moving disturbs the flower buds which may drop off unexpectedly, especially with subtle light or humidity changes. Over the years you will find your cactus will come back into bloom naturally each fall and again in spring. Fertilize the plants with a balanced, complete fertilizer in the summer and again in February and March.

Other gift plants like azaleas may also be brought back into bloom quite easily. Remember azaleas will lose most or all of their leaves gradually after Christmas. Keep the soil evenly moist and add cold tea occasionally to keep the soil acidic. In the summer, plunge the entire plant (pot and all) into a shady corner of the garden. Fertilize a few times and cut back any particularly long branches to keep the plant compact. Stop fertilizing in late August, bring the plant back indoors before frost, and wash it carefully to rinse off any bugs which may have been attracted to it in the outdoor garden. Top the soil up slightly and place in a medium light area. It doesn't need direct light. By late October or early November your azalea will be back in bloom for another two to three month season. Every branch tip will produce a flower bud.

How are poinsettias kept at their best for the longest time? Can you keep them in bloom or bring them back into bloom for next Christmas?

There are more than sixty-five different types of poinsettias sold in North America for the Christmas season. These plants are all hybrid clones from the Central and South American plant *Euphorbia pulcherrima*. They all have very fine root systems which dry out quickly because their tropical rainforest homeland habitat has constantly moist, but not stagnantly wet, soil. They really suffer from overwatering and salt damage which results from water sitting in the saucer and overfertilizing.

Poinsettias must be watched very closely and kept away from drafts both on their trip home from the store and once at home. To keep them blooming as long as possible give them a bright sunny windowsill. Watch for wilting due to overwatering or drying. If the colourful bracts begin to drop assume you are overfertilizing or overwatering or overheating your plant. If they have been stored too long in boxes in the warehouse or in shipping, the leaves may droop.

Poinsettia

Once all the colourful leaves (bracts) have dropped, cut the plant back by half and repot into a larger eight or ten inch pot. With a very high light and fertilizer regime during the summer, the plant will rebound and grow vigorously. Pinching out the fast growing tips a few times will keep the plant bushy. Remove lower shoots throughout the summer and most of the lower leaves just before forcing the plant to rebloom; this encourages a number of strong tall branches in the larger pot.

The plant must be given long nights for 70 days before it will bloom again at Christmas. Do this either by covering the plant with a box for 14 hours each night starting in late September; placing the pot in a cupboard; or by keeping the plant in a room with lights on a timer. Don't interrupt the dark period or you will delay bloom. Keep the temperature at 16-18 degrees Celsius during the forcing period. The simplest approach is to grow your well watered and fertilized plant along with your other houseplants and let it come naturally into bloom when the conditions are right - which is close to Christmas - if the plant only receives natural light.

What can you do about the tops of birch trees that are dying?

Not much. Birch need regular and continuous watering in the growing season with minimal pruning and absolutely no root disturbance. If the tops of your trees are dead, you could have simple drought or the more difficult bronze birch borer. Either way, prune off the dead growth as soon as you notice it and don't forget to water excessively, if necessary, next summer.

I have heard it is easy to compost with worms, specifically red worms. How can I get started?

We want to start a red worm box in our school to eat all the organic waste we produce. Do you know who we contact to obtain these worms?

Some of the best worms for vermiculture are the red wigglers (*Eisenia foetida*). Their preferred temperature is 25 degrees Celsius and they love rich organic soil with a near neutral pH. They like to be fed regularly which means you need to constantly place small pieces of vegetable matter in alternating corners of their box. They don't like onions, so don't add them to their box or you'll be removing them later! There are many mail-order sources. For availability check the classified ads in Canadian gardening magazines or write to:

The Wormletter
#202, 20 Cosburn Avenue
Toronto, Ontario
M4K 2E7
(Quarterly Newsletter; $6.00 per year)

What is the best way to care for your Christmas tree so that it lasts without dropping its needles before New Year's?

Believe it or not, the most success with keeping needles on fir trees in tests done by the North Carolina State University was with fresh water. Researchers compared fresh water with other solutions including commercial preservatives and "homemade" mixtures containing chlorox and aspirin.[63] I usually recommend buying a tree from an outside lot which is protected from wind and direct sun. Trees sold in warm buildings or sunny outdoor lots may dry out more than those kept frozen. Making

---

63. As reported in The Avant Gardener, P16, Vol 25, N0 2, December 1992.

a fresh cut on the bottom of the tree and placing it in water immediately after making the cut will help preserve freshness. Fir trees have the softest green needles and they are the best choice if you want fresh green needles for the entire season. Spruce and all pines, especially Scots pines, tend to dry more quickly. If in doubt, buy whatever is grown locally because it will be fresher.

Can I make my blue spruce more blue by nailing rusty spikes into it?

Can I make my blue spruce more blue by adding two cups of sugar to the base in the summer?

Blue spruce are like blondes. Colorado spruce which have been started from seed will be a variety of shades from dark green through to blue. The colour isn't exact or precise but is available in a range. The best blues have been "cloned" and one of the best clones is the Hoopsii blue spruce; one of the poorest shaped blue spruce clones is Koster blue spruce.

The blue on the blue spruce is just a waxy coating over the emerging leaves which protects the new leaves from the impact of high light at the high elevations where this spruce grows in mountainous Colorado. As the season wears on and the leaves become accustomed to the light, the blue waxy coating gradually washes off in the rain and snow. By the following spring, the blue on the old needles may be almost gone while the new, very blue needles are emerging. There isn't a single treatment, either sugar, or rusty nails which can change the genetics of your blue spruce trees.

Because blue spruce are genetically more or less blue, the best way to make sure you are getting the shade of blue you want (if you aren't wanting to spend the extra money to get a named clone) is to select the bluest one you can find in the nursery in the spring. The trees which hold their blue colour longest will still be blue in the spring before the new growth emerges.

Appendix:

Sources mentioned in the text:

B & D Lilies
(colour catalogues for this American supplier are available from a Canadian supplier):
Crescent Nursery,
RR #4,
Rockwood, ON,
Canada, N0B 2K0
Tel: (519)856-1000

The Cook's Garden
P.O. Box 535,
Londonderry, VT,
05148, USA
Tel: (802)824-3400
Fax#: (802)824-3027

Gardenimport Inc.
P.O. Box 760,
Thornhill, ON,
Canada, L3T 4A5
Tel: (905)731-1950
Fax: (905)881-3499

Hardy Roses of The North
Box 2048C,
Grand Forks, BC,
Canada, V0H 1H0
(Catalogue $2.00 refundable)

Honeywood Lilies
Box 63,
Parkside, SK,
Canada, S0J 2A0
Tel: (306)747-3296.
(Catalogue $2.00)

Hortico Roses
723 Robson Rd.,
Waterdown, ON,
Canada, L0R 2H1
Tel: (905)689-6984

Monashee Perennials
RR # 7, Site 6
Box 9,
Vernon, BC,
Canada, V1T 7Z3

Otto Richter & Sons (Herbs)
Box 26,
Goodwood, ON,
Canada, L0C 1A0
(Catalogue $2.50)

Parkland Perennials
Box 3683
Spruce Grove, AB,
Canada, T7X 3A9
Tel: (403)963-7307

Sprout Farms (Apple Trees)
Box 719,
Bon Accord, AB,
Canada, T0A 0K0
Fax: (403)921-3995

Stokes Seeds Ltd.
39 James St., Box 10,
St. Catherines, ON,
Canada, L2R 6R6

Tansy Farm
58888 Else Road,
Route 1,
Agassiz, BC,

Canada, V0M 1R0
(Catalogue $2.00)

Thompson and Morgan Inc.
P.O. Box 1308,
Jackson, NJ,
08527-0308 USA

McMillen's Iris Garden
RR 1,
Norwich, ON,
Canada, N0J 1P0
(Catalogue $2.00)

Moore Water Gardens
Port Stanley, ON,
Canada, N5L 1J4
(Free Catalogue)

Rainforest Gardens
13139 224 St., RR2
Maple Ridge, BC
V2X 7E7
Fax (604) 467-3181

White Flower Farm
Litchfield, CT,
06759-0050, USA
Tel: (203)496-9600.
(Free Catalogue)

Wrightman's Alpines
RR 3, Kerwood, ON,
Canada, N0M 2B0
(Catalogue $2.00)

**Composting and
Earthworm Information:**

**Composting Council of
Canada**
200 MacLaren Street,
Suite 300

Ottawa, ON,
Canada, K2P 0L6

The Wormletter
#202, 20 Cosburn Avenue
Toronto, ON,
Canada, M4K 2E7
(Quarterly Newsletter; $6.00
per year)

**Biological Controls and
Natural Methods:**

Green Methods Catalogue
Dept. Of Bio-Ingenuity
93 Priest Road
Barrington, NH,
03825, USA
Tel: (603)942-8925
Fax: (603)942-8932

**Phero Tech Inc. Pest
Management Specialists**
Wholesale supplier of
sticky traps.
Tel:(604)940-9944
(Call for a list of local suppli-
ers of their products)

**Specialty Plant Groups to
join for further information:**

**The Hoya Society
International, Inc.**
P.O. Box 1043HP
Porterdale, GO,
30270, USA
Membership: $25.00 (US
funds) per year

**Alberta Regional Lily
Society (ARLS)**
P.O. Box 3683
Spruce Grove, AB,

Canada, T7X 3A9
(Membership is $10.00 per
year)

CRAGS
Calgary Rock & Alpine
Garden Society
(A Chapter of the North
American Rock Garden Society)
Membership Inquiries:
c/o Sheila Paulson
6960 Leaside Drive SW
Calgary, AB,
Canada, T3E 6H5
(Membership is $7.00 per year
and includes a quarterly
newsletter, garden tours and
regular meetings)

North American Rock
Garden Society (NARGS)
Executive Secretary
P.O. Box 67
Millwood, NY 10546
($32 Canadian)

Lists:

Easy care "no sweat" perennials:
(few pests, no problems, rarely or never needing any transplanting or dividing)

- Astilbe hybrids - up late in the spring but wonderful all summer (*Astilbe* cvs.)
- Bergenia (*Bergenia cordifolia*)
- Blue Clips bluebells (*Campanula carpatica* 'Blue Clips')
- Blue fescue (*Festuca ovina* and cvs.)
- Coral bells (*Heuchera sanguinea*)
- Daylily (*Hemerocallis* cvs.)
- Dianthus (*Dianthus deltoides*)
- Drumstick primula (*Primula denticulata*)
- Dwarf pink baby's breath (*Gypsophila repens rosea*)
- Euphorbia (*Euphorbia polychroma* and *E. myrsinites*)
- Flax (*Linum perenne*)
- Gaillardia (*Gaillardia aristata* and 'Burgundy', 'Goblin' cvs.)
- Liatris (*Liatris spicata*)
- Peonies - make sure not to transplant more than once every forty years (*Paeonia* cvs.)
- Purple coneflower - Attracts butterflies to the late summer garden (*Echinaceae purpurea*)
- Shasta daisy (*Leucanthemum maximum* 'Snow Lady')
- Siberian iris (several cvs. *Iris sibirica*, especially 'Little Tricolor')
- Silver mound (*Artemesia schmidtiana*)

Touchable perennial plants:
(Plants for a sensory experience in a children's garden or near a sitting area)

- Lamb's ears (*Stachys byzantia* and *Stachys byzantia* 'Aurea')
- Silver mound (*Artemesia schmidtiana*)
- Silver brocade artemesia (*Artemesia stelleriana* 'Silver Brocade')

Annual flowers, perennials, and shrubs for hot spots:

- Basket-of-gold (*Aurinia saxatalis* 'compacta') - great for an early perennial spring splash of bright yellow. May die out quickly in some gardens but readily reseeds so look for it's grey-green leaves popping up here and there in the spring.
- Dahlberg daisy (*Dyssodia tenuifolia*) - annual yellow daisy but will self seed.
- Helianthemum (Sun Rose) - low growing hardy perennial plant in various shades of pink, orange, and yellow.
- Prairie coneflower (*Ratibida columnifera*) - native to the prairies with very beautiful yellow flowers in summer.
- All silver-leaved plants including perennial silvermound, silver brocade artemesia, and pussy-toes; shrubs such as native wolf willow *(Elaeagnus commutata)* and the orange berried common sea buckthorn (*Hippophae rhamnoides*); trees like the Russian olive (*Elaeagnus angustifolia*) and silver poplar (*Populus alba* 'Nivea'); annuals such as silverdust dusty miller.
- Several annual flowers such as: geraniums, annual pennisetum grass, calendula, flamingo feather wheat celosia, annual dianthus, bachelor's buttons, African daisy, strawflowers, sunflowers, lady lavender, larkspur, lavatera, marigold, nigella, petunia, portulaca, salvia, statice, and Livingstone daisy.
- Succulent plants such as sedums, saxifrages, hens & chicks.

Flowers for evening gardens:

- Plants with pale, white, or evening scented flowers will be dramatic at dusk.
- Daylilies (*Hemerocallis* cvs. - some bloom in the late afternoon and evening such as 'Stella de Oro').
- Evening scented stocks, nicotiana, and clary sage all smell sweet in the evening.
- Perennials with white blossoms such as white liatris (*Liatris spicata* 'Floristan'), white iris (Iris 'Winter Olympics'), white astilbe (*Astilbe* 'Bridal Veil'), white coneflower (*Echinacea* 'White Swan').
- Plants with white edged leaves including hostas, dogwoods, alpine lady's mantle, goutweed, lamium, physostegia, and weigela cvs. Look for the word "variegata" in the name somewhere.

Great groundcovers:

- Cliff green (*Paxistima canbyi*)
- Dwarf fleeceflower (*Polygonum affine* 'Pink Jewel')
- Horizontal juniper (*Juniperus horizontalis* 'Yukon Belle', J. h. 'Blue Chip')
- Iris moss, Scotch moss (*Sagina subulata, Sagina subulata* 'Aurea')
- Moss phlox (*Phlox subulata*)
- Pachysandra (*Pachysandra terminalis*)
- Periwinkle (*Vinca minor*)
- Pussytoes (*Antennaria rosea*)
- Red mother-of-thyme (*Thymus serpyllum* 'Coccineus')

Bedding plants (annuals) for the shade:

- Alyssum
- Begonias, non-stop
- Begonias, tuberous
- Coleus
- Fuschia
- Impatiens plant
- Kennelworth ivy
- Nasturtium
- Nicotiana
- Pansy

Perennials for the shade:

- Achillea: many kinds (*Achillea* cvs.)
- Balloon flower (*Platycodon grandiflorus*)
- Baneberry (*Actaea rubra*)
- Bellflower (*Campanula* sp.)
- Bergenia (*Bergenia cordifolia*)
- Bleeding heart - several kinds (*Dicentra* cvs.)
- Coral bells (*Heuchera* cvs.)
- Corydalis - yellow and blue flowered types (*Corydalis* cvs.)
- Creeping jenny (*Lysimachia* sp.)
- Ferns (many kinds)
- Foam flower (*Tiarella* sp.)
- Forget-me-not (*Myosotis* cvs.)
- Foxglove (*Digitalis* cvs.)

- Goutweed (*Aegopodium podagraria*)
- Hosta: many kinds especially the cream edged and white flowering types (*Hosta* cvs.)
- Lily-of-the-valley (*Convallaria majalis*)
- Lungwort: many kinds with white spotted leaves (*Pulmonaria* cvs.)
- Mint (*Mentha* cvs.)
- Pachysandra (*Pachysandra terminalis*)
- Perennial spirea (*Astilbe* cvs.)
- Primrose: many kinds, especially the vulgaris types (*Primula* cvs.)
- Solomon's seal (*Polygonatum multiforum*)
- Trollius (*Trollius* sp.)
- Windflower (*Anemone sylvestris*)

Glossary Of Terms

Annuals: plants started as seed and grown to maturity in one season. Must be replanted every year and includes many flowering plants such as petunias and geraniums in our climate. Some, but not all, annual plants may be grown as perennials in a warmer climate.

Balanced fertilizer: the three numbers on the package are about the same i.e., 20-20-20.

Beneficial insects: the "good guys" in the battle of the bugs. Beneficials might be parasites or predators on the other invertebrates who are eating or damaging our garden plants.

Biological controls: any natural agent for insect, weed or microorganism control.

Biorational: the green way to do things.

Branch collar: the ridge between the trunk of a tree and the branch coming off the trunk. This area protects the main trunk from disease if left intact during pruning. It is a different size and shape on each type of tree.

Chitting: presoaking seeds before planting.

Clone: a group of plants all having the identical genetic make up. Each and every plant that is cloned is identical and they all arise from a single plant which was reproduced vegetatively.

Complete fertilizer: has something in each part of the formula i.e., 15-20-10, not 0-10-10.

Cultivar (cv.): a cultivar might be, but is not necessarily, a hybrid or cross between two different plants. Some really good cultivars are cloned to produce identical plants. The term cultivar follows the species name of the plant, as in Campanula carpatica cv. 'Blue Chips'. The abbreviation for cultivar is 'cv.'.

Dormant oil: a light mineral or vegetable oil which is mixed with water and sprayed on plants late in the dormant season. This is a "biorational" insect spray, which is also useful for controlling some fungi when mixed with sulphur.

213

Floating row cover: see Reemay and polyester row cover.

Flower spur: a small twig on a plant where flower buds are formed. Apple and Hoya are two different plants with flowers on obvious spurs.

Forcing bulbs: bringing bulbous plants into bloom before nature would. This allows us to have colourful tulips and daffodils in bloom months ahead of time indoors.

Genus: like a person's last name, the genus name tells you what group a plant fits in to. The genus name is always italicised or underlined, and is capitalized. Expect similarities among plants from the same genus (i.e., *Primula).*

Goofless gardening: it can't be done. We are all really still learning and when we exchange ideas we all benefit.

Growth regulator: a product designed to keep plants in the greenhouse short and compact.

Integrated growth management (IGM): involves benign pest control as well as all other factors contributing to the health of plants... soil, site, plant selection and cultural methods.

Integrated pest management (IPM): look before you spray and then spray or treat with the most environmentally sound method which might be soap or might be a biological such as a predatory mite.

Larva/larvae: the second phase in an insect's complete life cycle. First comes the egg, then comes the larva. More than one larva is two larvae.

Nematode: small invertebrate, but not a true insect. Usually worm-like and either a pest in warmer climates or a valuable biological control in our cool climate.

Open pollinated: seeds are formed from crosses between related and unrelated plants in an open field situation.

Peat moss: shredded sphagnum moss from northern bogs. The world's best peat comes from Canada and the gardener's favorite type of peat is coarsely shredded because it doesn't blow away as easily.

Perennials: plants that regrow from the same root year after year even though the topgrowth dies back in the fall. Some perennials flower but many are grown for their interesting leaves and texture.

Pinching: the act of picking off the new pair of leaves at the top or outer edge of a branch. This removes the growing point and encourages sprouting from lower buds or branches.

Pine candles: the spring emerging leaf buds on pines come out as long thin, orange spires in May. These growths, called candles, gradually expand to reveal the new flush of growth.

Polyester row cover: also called Reemay or floating row cover.

Pruning paint/tar: material used to hide or disguise a pruning cut without any benefit but some obvious detriment if used.

Reemay: the brand name for one of the polyester fabrics used to extend the growing season and to protect plants from insect damage.

Species: the second name in the "Latin" name. It follows right after the genus name and it gives more information about the plant. (i.e., *Fraxinus mandschurica* - the species name mandschurica indicates that this "Fraxinus" is from Manchuria - logically, the common name is Manchurian ash).

Suckers: the same as water sprouts; these are often caused by planting a tree too deep or by pruning too heavily in the dormant season.

Systemic chemical: a chemical which works by moving up through the tree from the bark or the roots and into the leaves, where it ultimately kills the insects it is targeted for as they eat the plant's leaves.

Tanglefoot: A tradename for a sticky product used to physically trap insects. Comes in tubes and rolls.

Tree topping: cutting back a tree in an unnatural way to shorten it. Frequently done to poplars in the winter.

Tuber: a fleshy root, usually with buds, which is actually a swollen underground stem usually treated as a bulb. Potatoes and dahlias are examples of tubers.

Water sprouts: The long straight upright branches which grow from the ground or from horizontal branches on trees. They are a sign that the tree is under stress.

Wildflowers: technically these are native plants, but this term is now broadly used to mean native plants from anywhere in the world which are mixed together in "wildflower" blends.

Index

219

$\mathcal{T}$o order additional copies of Gardening for Goofs please mail your cheque or money order payable to:

No Sweat Gardening Inc.

$19.95 plus $3.00 shipping and handling and 7% GST ($24.56 total) per book to:

No Sweat Gardening Inc
BOX 46021, INGLEWOOD P.O.
CALGARY, AB T2G 5H7

Name: _____

Address: _____

Town/City: _____

Postal Code: _____

Number of books ordered: ___ Total Payment Enclosed: _____

Please allow 2-4 weeks for delivery.

No Sweat Gardening Inc
BOX 46021, INGLEWOOD P.O.
CALGARY, AB T2G 5H7

Name: _____

Address: _____

Town/City: _____

Postal Code: _____

Number of books ordered: ___ Total Payment Enclosed: _____

Please allow 2-4 weeks for delivery.

No Sweat Gardening Inc
BOX 46021, INGLEWOOD P.O.
CALGARY, AB T2G 5H7

Name: _____

Address: _____

Town/City: _____

Postal Code: _____

Number of books ordered: ___ Total Payment Enclosed: _____

Please allow 2-4 weeks for delivery.